STUDY GUIDE TO ACCOMPANY

Computers!

Third Edition

DIANE KRASNEWICH • TIMOTHY N. TRAINOR

Mitchell McGRAW-HILL
New York St. Louis San Francisco Auckland Bogotá Caracas Hamburg
Lisbon London Madrid Mexico Milan Montreal New Delhi Paris
San Juan São Paulo Singapore Sydney Tokyo Toronto Watsonville

Mitchell **McGRAW-HILL**
Watsonville, CA 95076

Study Guide to Accompany Computers! Third Edition

Copyright © 1992 by **McGraw-Hill, Inc.** All rights reserved. Printed in the United States of America. Except as permitted under the United States Copyright Act of 1976, no part of this publication may be reproduced or distributed in any form or by any means, or stored in a database or retrieval system, without the prior written permission of the publisher.

1 2 3 4 5 6 7 8 9 0 MAL MAL 9 0 9 8 7 6 5 4 3 2 1

ISBN 0-07-035223-2

The editor was Erika Berg.
The editorial assistant was Denise Nickeson.
The cover designer was Christy Butterfield.

TABLE OF CONTENTS

Preface v

Unit 1: Putting Information Technology To Work

    Chapter 1 1
    Chapter 2 15
    Chapter 3 31

Unit 2: Personal Productivity Tools

    Chapter 4 45
    Chapter 5 63
    Chapter 6 81
    Chapter 7 93
    Chapter 8 105

Unit 3: Hardware and Communications

    Chapter 9 121
    Chapter 10 137
    Chapter 11 157

Unit 4: Information Systems

    Chapter 12 173
    Chapter 13 187
    Chapter 14 205

Unit 5: Technological Trends

    Chapter 15 219
    Chapter 16 231

Appendix A 247

Appendix B 255

Appendix C 265

Appendix D 271

PREFACE

USING COMPUTERS! 3e AS A LEARNING TOOL

This Study Guide is designed to help you better understand the material found in *Computers!* Third Edition. The Guide is broken down into chapters that correspond to the chapters in the textbook. Each chapter is organized into eight sections. Let's review what the sections are and their purposes.

PURPOSE - The purpose is a brief statement about the central focus of the chapter and the main ideas covered within it. It will give you an idea of what is to come.

TERMS TO REMEMBER - A list is included of all the important terms that are boldfaced in the text. Definitions for these terms can also be found in the Glossary.

ANSWERS TO REVIEW QUESTIONS - Space is provided to answer the review questions found at the end of each chapter. Answers to all the review questions are found in the text. These questions will help when studying for tests.

PROJECTS - Suggested class/homework assignments are described in detail. These projects are different from the "Applying What You've Learned" exercises described in the text. Many of the projects correspond to the worksheets discussed in the next section.

Some of the projects start with "WHAT DO YOU THINK?" They are designed to be thought-provoking and may not have a single clear-cut answer. These projects cover the effects computers may have on your life -- both good and bad.

WORKSHEETS - The worksheets are used in association with selected projects. Worksheets are placed at the end of each chapter in this guide. They can be written on and handed in if assigned. Each worksheet has, at the top, the related chapter and project number.

MIX AND MATCH - Since a large part of any introduction to computer technology requires learning terms and definitions, each chapter contains a mix and match exercise. Write the letter from the associated term in the blank space in front of the definition. Your instructor has the correct answers.

CROSSWORD PUZZLES - As another way to test your knowledge of the chapter's important terms, you could do the crossword puzzle included in this Guide. It contains most of the Terms To Remember for a chapter as well as some terms from previous chapters. See your instructor for the correct answers to the crossword puzzles.

REFERENCES - The references provide a listing of additional sources of information about the material contained in the chapters. These can be useful to you when researching answers to the "Applying What you've Learned" and Study Guide projects.

Studying the chapters in the text by using this Study Guide will help you understand more about computers and how they can be used. Regardless of what you do in the future, your life will be touched by computers. Make the most of it!

                                        Diane Krasnewich
                                       Timothy N. Trainor
                                       Muskegon, Michigan

CHAPTER 1: END-USER COMPUTING

PURPOSE

This chapter introduces the Input-Processing-Output-Storage cycle, a basic pattern found in all computer applications. The types of data and processing a computer can do as well as general applications are discussed. Also the capabilities and limits in using computer technology are explored.

TERMS TO REMEMBER

arithmetic operation	logical operation
computer	numeric data
computer application	physical data
computer program	process control
data	programmable
database	simulation
data processing	text
data storage and retrieval	textual data
embedded computer	transaction
end-user	user friendly
icon	

ANSWERS TO REVIEW QUESTIONS

1. Define each "term to remember".

   arithmetic operation -

   computer -

   computer application -

   computer program -

   data -

1

database -

data processing -

data storage and retrieval -

embedded computer -

end-user -

icon -

logical operation -

numeric data -

physical data -

process control -

programmable -

simulation -

text -

textual data -

transaction -

user friendly -

2. Provide an example of each of the following tasks computers perform everyday: process control, simulations, data storage and retrieval, and data processing.

process control -

Example:

simulations -

Example:

data storage and retrieval -

Example:

data processing -

Example:

3. What is the four-step cycle used by computers and other tools?

    1.

    2.

    3.

    4.

4. What are three types of data computers can use as input?

    1.

    2.

    3.

5. What are two ways in which calculators and computers are similar and two ways in which they are different?

    Similar:

    1.

    2.

    Different:

    1.

    2.

6. Describe two processing operations that computers perform.

    1.

    2.

7. Why do embedded computers make tools more flexible?

End-User Computing

8. What are five ways in which computers increase the capacity of people to control their environment?

   1.

   2.

   3.

   4.

   5.

9. What is the chief limitation of computer technology?

10. List four activities that computers cannot perform.

    1.

    2.

    3.

    4.

11. List four general activities that computers can do well.

    1.

    2.

    3.

    4.

12. Why should people avoid giving up decision-making responsibilities to computers?

13. What are four misunderstandings that people have about computer technology?

    1.

    2.

    3.

    4.

14. Identify eight questions and answers new **end-users** often ask.

    1.

    2.

    3.

    4.

    5.

    6.

    7.

    8.

PROJECTS

1. Complete WORKSHEET #1.1 and hand it in to your instructor. This questionnaire will help the instructor know the kinds of computer experience you have and your expectations for the class.

2. Collect and read a computer-related article or advertisement from a newspaper or magazine. List the words you don't understand. Add to this list as you see new words throughout the course, crossing off words as you learn their meaning.

3. Use WORKSHEET #1.2 to list five IPOS cycles that you use inside or outside of school. Show examples different from those mentioned in the text. Be able to relate input, processing, output, and storage ideas to your examples. The examples *do not* have to be computer related.

4. WHAT DO YOU THINK? Some people in the country do not know very much about technology.
   - What are some ways outside of a classroom that they could learn more?
   - Do you think it is important to know about technology if you are retired or not working?
   - At what age should a person start learning about computers?

5. WHAT DO YOU THINK? Computers sometimes have a bad reputation. They are accused of putting people out of work and being far too complicated for "ordinary people" to understand.
   - What are your opinions of how computers fit into society?
   - Could you get along without them?
   - Upon what experiences are your opinions based?

WORKSHEETS

1.1 Student questionnaire

1.2 IPOS cycle related to five examples you have seen
    (They do not have to be computer related)

REFERENCES

Arnold, David O. *Impact! Computers and Society*. New York: Mitchell McGraw-Hill, 1991.

de Jong, Ton. "Learning and instruction with computer simulation", *Education and Computing*, vol. 6, no. 3/4, pp. 217-229.

Gow, Kathleen A. "No thanks, I can do it by myself". *Computerworld*, May 30, 1991, p. 98.

O'Leary, Timothy, et al. *Computing Essentials*. New York: Mc-Graw Hill, 1989.

Pastore, Richard. "Beyond the beginner's slope". *Computerworld*, May 20, 1991, p. 96.

Rifkin, Glenn. "End-user training: Needs improvement." *Computerworld*, April 15, 1991, pp. 73-74.

Wohl, Amy D. (Ed.) *The Wohl Report on End-user Computing*. Bala Cynwyd, PA: Wohl Associates (newsletter).

End-User Computing

MIX AND MATCH

Match the following terms with the definitions below.
Each question has only one answer.

a. arithmetic operation
b. computer
c. computer application
d. computer program
e. data
f. database
g. data processing
h. data storage and retrieval
i. embedded computer
j. end-user
k. icon

l. logical operation
m. numeric data
n. physical data
o. process control
p. programmable
q. simulation
r. text
s. textual data
t. transaction
u. user friendly

_____ 1. instructions for a computer

_____ 2. computer built into a tool

_____ 3. capable of having program instructions changed

_____ 4. machine that processes facts and figures

_____ 5. holding and searching through vast amounts of data

_____ 6. numbers, decimal points as data

_____ 7. using a computer to monitor and adjust an activity

_____ 8. operation dealing with the comparison of data

_____ 9. letters, punctuation as data

_____ 10. operation dealing with numerical computation

_____ 11. using the computer to convert facts and figures into useful information

_____ 12. pictures representing information

_____ 13. the facts and figures put into a computer

_____ 14. computer mimics a real life situation

_____ 15. use for a computer

_____ 16. data obtained from the environment

_____ 17. exchange of value

_____ 18. person who uses a computer to solve problems and organize data

_____ 19. large collection of cross-referenced information

_____ 20. computers that are easy to use

_____ 21. another name for textual data

Chapter 1

by A. Walters

ACROSS

1. Data ____ ____ ____, computers are used to store vast amounts of data and search for relevant reference material. (3 words)
5. Use for a computer, computer ____.
6. ____ operation ability of a computer to do mathematical functions.
11. ____ data, numbers, decimal point, plus sign, and negative sign.
13. ____ control, where a computer caoconstantly monitors and adjusts an activity.
14. Computer built inside a tool. (2 words)
17. Exchange of value.
18. ____ data, any combination of letters, numbers or special characters.
19. Another name for textual data.
20. Data from the environment. (2 words)
21. Computer ____, the set of instructions a computer follows in sequence to control the input, processing, output, and storage it is to perform.

DOWN

1. A computer-generated environment that mimics a real life or imaginary situation.
2. Person who can use technology to organize data, stimulate ideas, solve problems and communicate the results to others.
3. Ability of a computer to compare two values (larger, smaller). (2 words, with 16 down)
4. Facts and figures.
7. Picture of items on a keyboard.
8. Machine that allows input of facts and figures, processes them, and outputs useful information.
9. Using a computer to convert facts and figures into useful information. (2 words)
10. The ability of computers and some calculators to follow a stored sequence of instruction for processing input.
12. An attribute of computers meaning easy to use. (2 words)
15. Organized collections of data that can be retrieved and cross-referenced by a computer.
16. (last half of 3 down)

CHAPTER 1

WORKSHEET 1.1   Name:_____

PLEASE ANSWER THESE QUESTIONS AS COMPLETELY AS YOU CAN. BE SPECIFIC. THE INFORMATION YOU PROVIDE WILL HELP ME SET UP THE CLASS ACCORDING TO YOUR NEEDS AND PAST EXPERIENCES.

1. WHY ARE YOU TAKING THIS CLASS?
   (recommended by advisor, required for major, interested in computers, etc.)

2. WHAT DO YOU EXPECT TO LEARN FROM THIS CLASS?

3. HAVE YOU HAD ANY EXPERIENCE USING COMPUTERS? ☐ YES ☐ NO
   IF SO, WHAT DID YOU DO AND WHAT KIND OF EQUIPMENT DID YOU USE?

4. ARE ANY COMPUTERS AVAILABLE TO YOU OUTSIDE OF SCHOOL? ☐ YES ☐ NO
   IF SO, WHAT KIND OF COMPUTER IS IT? HOW OFTEN IS IT AVAILABLE?

5. DO YOU HAVE ANY RELATIVES OR FRIENDS THAT WORK WITH COMPUTERS?
   IF SO, WHAT DO THEY THEY DO?

End-User Computing

WORKSHEET: 1.2
PROJECT: 3

Name: _____

IPOS CYCLE DESCRIPTION	INPUT	PROCESSING	OUTPUT	STORAGE
1.				
2.				
3.				
4.				
5.				

CLASS NOTES

CHAPTER 2: TECHNOLOGICAL PROGRESS

PURPOSE

This chapter traces the history of computing machines from ancient times through the fifth generation. Each new technological development is seen as a solution to an information problem.

TERMS TO REMEMBER

application generator
artificial intelligence (AI)
assembly language
batch processing
binary code
bit
card punch
card reader
chip
fourth-generation language (4GL)
hardware
high-level language
integrated circuits (IC)
keypunch
machine language
mainframe

microcomputer
microprocessor
minicomputer
multitasking
network
offline
online processing
operating system
optical computer
parallel processing
personal productivity
software
software
supercomputer
superconductor

INFORMATION TECHNOLOGY PIONEERS

Howard G. Aiken
John V. Atanasoff
Charles Babbage
John Bardeen
J. Georg Bednorz
Clifford Berry
George Boole
Walter Brattain
Seymour Cray
J. Presper Eckert
Adele Goldstein
Marcian (Ted) Hoff
Herman Hollerith

Grace Hopper
Gilbert Hyatt
Joseph Marie Jacquard
Steve Jobs
Jack Kilby
Ada Lovelace
John W. Mauchley
K. Alex Muller
Blaise Pascal
William Shockley
John von Neumann
Steve Wozniak

15

CHAPTER 2

ANSWERS TO REVIEW QUESTIONS

1. Define each "term to remember".

   application generator -

   artificial intelligence (AI) -

   assembly language -

   batch processing -

   binary code -

   bit (binary digit) -

   card punch -

   card reader -

   chip -

fourth generation language -

hardware -

high-level language -

integrated circuits (IC) -

keypunch -

machine language -

mainframe -

microcomputer -

microprocessor -

minicomputer -

multitasking-

network -

offline -

online processing -

operating system -

optical computer -

parallel processing -

personal productivity software -

software -

supercomputer -

Technological Progress

superconductor -

2. Describe the contribution each "information technology pioneer" made.

Howard G. Aiken -

John V. Atanasoff -

Charles Babbage -

John Bardeen -

J. Georg Bednorz -

Clifford Berry -

George Boole -

Walter Brattain -

Seymour Cray -

J. Presper Eckert -

Adele Goldstein -

Marcian (Ted) Hoff -

Herman Hollerith -

Grace Hopper -

Gilbert Hyatt -

Joseph Marie Jacquard -

Steve Jobs -

Jack Kilby -

Ada Lovelace -

John W. Mauchley -

K. Alex Muller -

Blaise Pascal -

Technological Progress

William Shockley -

John von Neumann -

Steve Wozniak -

3. What is the relationship between problems and technical solutions?

4. Why did early computer systems use punched cards for storage?

5. How are a keypunch, card reader, and card punch related to punched card processing?

6. How did the passage of social security legislation affect demand for computing equipment?

7. What were the main characteristics of first-generation computers and software?

21

8. What features of second-generation computers and software distinguished them from the first generation?

9. What is one advantage of working offline?

10. What are the characteristic features of third-generation computers and software?

11. What is one advantage of multitasking?

12. What are the characteristic features of fourth generation computers and software?

Technological Progress

13. Identify four types of personal productivity software.

   1.

   2.

   3.

   4.

14. Why are fourth-generation languages called application generators?

15. What are the major characteristics of fifth-generation hardware?

16. How is it possible to make computers faster?

17. What are two human attributes that would be difficult to duplicate with artificial intelligence?

   1.

   2.

18. How will special-purpose processors add more power to new computer systems?

CHAPTER 2

PROJECTS

1. Use the text and any additional sources to fill out the Generation Chart on WORKSHEET 2.1. For each of the five generations, list the relevant facts. Not all of the boxes can be filled in, or may require some additional research. There may also be some overlap in some categories.

   HARDWARE:

   a) How was the information processed in the computer (tubes, transistors, etc.)?
   b) What were the names of the most famous computers?

   PROGRAMS:

   a) How were the computer instructions stored? What kind of programming languages were used?
   b) How many programs could the computer handle at one time?

   DATA:

   a) For what kinds of data (or applications) were these computers used?
   b) What were the forms or methods of input and output?
   c) How was the data stored?

   PEOPLE:

   a) Who were the people contributing the most at this time? Also identify what they contributed.
   b) Who were the users at this time?

2. Talk to someone who has worked with computers for over 15 years. Ask them what changes they've seen during that time. How have they been able to adjust to these changes through education and training? Write a short report on what you have discovered.

3. WHAT DO YOU THINK? Several people claim to be the inventor of the first electronic computer. Even lawsuits have been filed in this area. Do a short paper on who was the "father of the electronic computer." A basis for research is the two articles by Atanasoff and Mauchley mentioned in the References. Also, check the *Computer Literature Index* for more recent references.

Technological Progress

WORKSHEETS

2.1 Computer generations

REFERENCES

Atanasoff, John V. "Who invented the electronic general purpose digital computer?" *Computerworld*, July 9, 1984.

Babbage, Henry P., ed. *Babbage's Calculating Engine*. Reproduction of 1889 edition. Tomash Publications.

Baum, Joan. *The Calculating Power of Ada (Lovelace) Byron*. Hamden, CT: Archon Books, 1986.

Behar, Richard. "Who Invented Microprocessors?" *Time*, September 10, 1990.

Berry, Jean R. "Clifford Edward Berry. 1918-1963. His role in early computers." *Annals of the History of Computing*, October 1986, pp. 361-369.

Ceruzzi, Paul E. *Reckoners: The Prehistory of the Digital Computer, from Relays to the Stored Program Concept, 1935-1945*. Greenwood Press, 1984.

Cortada, James W. (compiled by). *A Bibliographic Guide to the History of Computing, Computers, and the Information Processing Industry*. Westport, CT: Greenwood Press, 1990.

Dubbey, J. M. *The Mathematical Work of Charles Babbage*. New York: Cambridge University Press, 1978.

Goldstine, Herman H. *The Computer from Pascal to Von Neumann*. Princeton, NJ: Princeton University Press, 1980.

Lichnewski, A. and Sague, Z. C. *Supercomputing: State of the Art*. Netherlands: Elsevier Science Publishers, 1987.

Lindren, Michael. *Glory and Failure*. Cambridge, MA: MIT Press, 1990.

Mauchley, Kathleen. "Who invented the electronic general purpose digital computer?" *Computerworld*, July 9, 1984.

Stein, Dorothy. *Ada: A Life and Legacy*. Cambridge, MA: MIT Press, 1985.

Sullivan-Trainor, Michael. "ENIAC, where are you now? Pieces of it are still working." *Computerworld*, November 3, 1986, p. 191.

MIX AND MATCH

Match the following terms with the definitions below.
Each question has only one answer.

I. PEOPLE

a. Aiken
b. Atanasoff and Berry
c. Babbage
d. Bardeen, Schockley, & Brattin
e. Bednorz and Muller
f. Boole
g. Cray
h. Goldstein
i. Hoff and Hyatt
j. Hopper
k. Hollerith
l. Jacquard
m. Jobs and Wozniak
n. Kilby
o. Lovelace
p. Mauchley and Eckert
q. Pascal
r. von Neumann

_____ 1. made first mechanical adding machine

_____ 2. designed difference engine, analytical engine

_____ 3. developed the integrated circuit

_____ 4. translated and annotated Babbage's work

_____ 5. developed two-state algebra

_____ 6. used punched cards to run a loom

_____ 7. used punched cards to store census data

_____ 8. developed MARK I

_____ 9. designed ENIAC

_____ 10. first programmer for MARK I

_____ 11. first programmer for ENIAC

_____ 12. completed electronic computer preceding ENIAC

_____ 13. his ideas included memory unit for storing program and data

_____ 14. discovered the properties of superconductors

_____ 15. developed Apple computer

Technological Progress

_____ 16. developed the transistor

_____ 17. pioneered development of the supercomputer

_____ 18. separately worked on the early microprocessors

II. TERMS AND CONCEPTS

a. application generator
b. artificial intelligence (AI)
c. assembly language
d. batch processing
e. binary code
f. bit
g. card punch
h. card reader
i. chip
j. fourth-generation language (4GL)
k. hardware
l. heuristic
m. high-level language
n. integrated circuits (IC)
o. keypunch
p. machine language

q. mainframe
r. microcomputer
s. microprocessor
t. minicomputer
u. multitasking
v. network
w. offline
x. online processing
y. operating system
z. optical computer
aa. parallel processing
bb. personal productivity software
cc. software
dd. supercomputer
ee. superconductor

_____ 1. binary digits

_____ 2. pattern of bits

_____ 3. punches holes in cards when person uses keyboard

_____ 4. translates punched cards into input data

_____ 5. punches output data onto card

_____ 6. computers and associated equipment

_____ 7. another name for computer programs

_____ 8. programming language in binary code

_____ 9. another name for fourth generation language

_____ 10. programming language using abbreviations for binary code

CHAPTER 2

_____ 11. input/output done remote from computers

_____ 12. processing data in large groups

_____ 13. another name for integrated circuit

_____ 14. programming languages using English words

_____ 15. material that loses electrical resistance at set temperatures

_____ 16. programs controlling computer hardware

_____ 17. computer runs several programs at same time

_____ 18. direct input of data into computer

_____ 19. large computer serving many users at the same time

_____ 20. computer powerful like mainframe, but smaller

_____ 21. processing equipment for third generation

_____ 22. computer based on microprocessor

_____ 23. fastest computer for handling complex applications

_____ 24. software packages for individual use

_____ 25. system of computers and peripherals connected by communication lines

_____ 26. easy-to-use programming languages

_____ 27. software simulating human thought

_____ 28. fifth-generation problem-solving technique

_____ 29. simultaneous use of several processors

_____ 30. computer using optical switches fibers in processing hardware

_____ 31. processing hardware characteristic of fourth generation

Chapter 2

by A. Walters

ACROSS

1. A small, personal computer whose processing basis is the microprocessor.
5. Machine that punches holes, representing data, onto punched cards. (2 words)
6. Machine operated through a keyboard that puts patterned holes on punch cards representing data.
8. Programming language that resembles human language more than machine (binary) language.
10. Material that loses all electrical resistance at a set temperature.
12. Solid state circuit placed with other electronic components on a silicon wafer. (abbr.)
13. ____ processing, simultaneous processing of several parts of the same program.
14. Software use that simulates human thought and judgement by use of heuristic problem solving. (abbr.)
15. ____ processing, processing large groups of data to maximize a computer's use.
16. ____ processing, direct input of data into a computer resulting in immediate response.
19. (second half of 21 across)
21. Pattern of on/off bits used to represent characters or operations in computer memory. (2 words, with 19 across)
22. (second half of 11 down)
23. Large computers with many users and connection to a variety of peripherals.
24. Work done while not connected to a computer.
25. ____ language, nonprocedural programming languages where users indicate IPOS requirements. (2 words)

DOWN

1. A single chip with input/output control, processing and memory circuitry.
2. Device that reads and translates holes on a punched card. (2 words)
3. ____ language, operating language unique to each computer, made up of bits.
4. Also known as fourth generation language. (2 words)
7. ____ intelligence, same as 14 across.
9. Computer and other equipment associated with a system.
10. A large, powerful high speed computer capable of handling large amounts of data.
11. Programs that help people with personal applications. (2 words, with 22 across)
17. Programs or instructions for the IPOS of data.
18. System of computers and peripherals sharing data and programs over communication lines.
20. ____ computer, processing hardware using optical fibers to transmit data internally for more speed.

WORKSHEET: 2.1
PROJECT: 1

Name:_____

	FIRST GENERATION	SECOND GENERATION	THIRD GENERATION	FOURTH GENERATION	FIFTH GENERATION
HARDWARE					
PROGRAMS					
DATA					
PEOPLE					

CHAPTER 3: COMPUTER INFORMATION SYSTEMS

PURPOSE

The five components of a computer system (people, procedures, data, software, and hardware) are introduced in this chapter. Their interrelationship with the IPOS cycle and importance to the computer system are examined through specific examples.

TERMS TO REMEMBER

boot
character
computer center manager
computer professional
computer system
crash
database program
diagnostic software
disk drive
disk operating system (DOS)
electronic spreadsheet
field
file
GIGO
graphics package
memory

mouse
operations personnel
peripheral
printer
procedure
processor
programmer
record
system
systems software
systems analyst
tape drive
user-developer
video display terminal (VDT)
word processing program

ANSWERS TO REVIEW QUESTIONS

1. Define each "term to remember".

    boot -

    character -

    computer center manager -

31

CHAPTER 3

computer professional -

computer system -

crash -

database program -

diagnostic software -

disk drive -

disk operating system (DOS) -

electronic spreadsheet -

field -

file -

Computer Information Systems

GIGO -

graphics package -

memory -

mouse -

operations personnel -

peripheral -

printer -

procedure -

processor -

programmer -

record -

system -

systems software -

systems analyst -

tape drive -

user-developer -

video display terminal (VDT) -

word processing program -

2. What are the five components of a computer system?

   1.   4.

   2.   5.

   3.

Computer Information Systems

3. What career options are available to computer professionals?

4. Identify one type of input hardware, processing hardware, output hardware, and storage hardware.

   Input hardware:

   Processing hardware:

   Output hardware:

   Storage hardware:

5. Describe the functions and type of data used for each of these application programs:

   word processing -

   electronic spreadsheet -

   graphics -

   database -

6. Describe the difference between systems software and application software.

7. Describe the three types of data.

   1.

   2.

   3.

8. What three characteristics must data have for successful completion of the IPOS cycle?

   1.

   2.

   3.

9. How is verification different from error correction?

10. What is included in each of these procedures:

    operating procedures -

    data entry procedures -

    error recovery procedures -

    preventive maintenance procedures -

    backup procedures -

    emergency procedures -

    troubleshooting procedures -

PROJECTS

1. Notice that the IPOS cycle can be applied to each of the five computer system components. Think of a place where you have seen computers used. It could be a business, store, library, etc. Try to analyze the application by filling in each of the 20 combinations found on WORKSHEET 3.1. If you don't know the correct terminology, describe what you think is involved. It is likely that not all of the 20 compartments can be used.

2. List three jobs related to computer operations. For each position, describe what is involved for each component of the computer system model.

3. Classify each computer application below by describing the input and output data. Also state the type of input and output data involved: numeric, text, or physical. In some cases, more than one type of data may be used. Complete WORKSHEET 3.2 for this assignment.

   a. admitting and later billing a hospital patient
   b. using a scanner to calculate a grocery bill
   c. a computer embedded within a car to operate the ignition system
   d. obtaining concert tickets through a computer-based reservation system
   e. the computer in a video game

4. Research in depth the use of computers in a specific area, possibly one that relates to your career plans. Use WORKSHEET 3.3 to organize that information as it relates to the five-component model of a computer system. Later, this worksheet will be the basis for a written report.

5. WHAT DO YOU THINK? Some people say "If at first it doesn't work, read the instructions!" Often, procedures and operating instructions for using computers are ignored until problems occur. How could people be persuaded to read the procedures for operating a computer before they start? How could this be implemented in a computer lab?

WORKSHEETS

3.1 Chart cross-matching five system components with four elements of the IPOS cycle

3.2 Classifying computer applications by type of input and output data

3.3 Organizing research done on the use of computers in a specific field of interest

REFERENCES

Biermann, Alan W. *Great Ideas in Computer Science: A Gentle Introduction.* Cambridge, MA: MIT Press, 1990.

Caron, Jeremiah. "More punch per dollar spent", *Computerworld*, May 20, 1991, p. 104.

Farnham, Alan. "The PC you put in your pocket", *Fortune*, May 20, 1991, pp. 113-114.

Grauer, Robert and Sugrue, Paul. *Microcomputer Applications.* New York: Mitchell McGraw-Hill, 1991.

Kroenke, David and Kathleen A. Dolan. *Business Computer Systems: An Introduction* (4rd ed.). New York: Mitchell McGraw-Hill Publishing, 1990.

Volinhals, O. *Elsevier's Dictionary of Personal and Office Computing in English, German, French, Italian, and Portuguese.* Netherlands: Elsevier Publishing, 1984.

Ward, Michael. *Software That Works.* Troy, MO: Academic Press, 1990.

Webster's New World Editorial Staff. *Webster's New World Dictionary of Computer Terms.* Englewood Cliffs, NJ: Prentice-Hall, 1988.

Computer Information Systems

MIX AND MATCH

Match the following terms with the definitions below.
Each question has only one answer.

a. boot
b. character
c. computer center manager
d. computer professional
e. computer system
f. crash
g. database
h. database program
i. diagnostic software
j. disk drive
k. disk operating system
l. electronic spreadsheet
m. field
n. file
o. GIGO
p. graphics package
q. memory
r. mouse
s. operations personnel
t. peripheral
u. printer
v. procedure
w. processor
x. programmer
y. record
z. system
aa. system software
bb. systems analyst
cc. tape drive
dd. user-developer
ee. VDT
ff. word processing program

_____ 1. people, data, hardware, software, procedures

_____ 2. hardware which displays information on a screen

_____ 3. people responsible for daily IPOS cycles

_____ 4. hardware for input/output/storage

_____ 5. hardware which displays information on paper

_____ 6. person supervising entire computer center

_____ 7. hardware to store data on tape

_____ 8. a single letter, number, symbol

_____ 9. a data item

_____ 10. hardware to store data on disk

_____ 11. related group of fields

_____ 12. user who knows some computer programming

_____ 13. related group of records

CHAPTER 3

_____ 14. program that cross-references files

_____ 15. person whose job focus is working directly with computers

_____ 16. program to generate pictures and drawings

_____ 17. accurate results depend on accurate input

_____ 18. hardware rolled on a flat surface, its movements becoming input

_____ 19. person working with user to develop computer system

_____ 20. temporary storage for data and programs

_____ 21. person who writes and tests programs

_____ 22. program to organize numeric data into rows and columns

_____ 23. interprets program, does arithmetic/logic

_____ 24. collection of elements working together

_____ 25. programs to operate computer system

_____ 26. systematic course of action

_____ 27. placing system software into the memory unit

_____ 28. program to create and edit text

_____ 29. collection of interrelated files

_____ 30. computer failure

_____ 31. program used in troubleshooting to find errors

_____ 32. system software booted from a disk

Chapter 3

by A. Walters

ACROSS

1. People whose job is the development and operation of computer technology. (pl) (2 words)
8. Unit in a computer that interprets software, controls memory, etc.
9. Hardware that makes magnetic tape available for reading, writing, and storage. (2 words, with 13 across)
10. Storage hardware that makes available data stored on disks. (2 words)
12. Failure of a computer system.
13. (second half of 9 across)
15. Operating system for microcomputers on disks. (abbr.)
16. ____ system, software that controls operations of computer regardless of applications being processed.
21. To load a systems program into memory in order to start up the computer.
23. Output hardware that provides permanent copy on paper.
24. Part of computer that is temporary storage.
25. Textual and numeric data organized by relationship of user access and analysis.
27. "Garbage in, garbage out."
29. Software that helps the user to create and store pictures, graphics, and diagrams. (2 words)

DOWN

1. Person responsible for equipment and workers in a computer center. (3 words)
2. Systematic course of action to help with software, hardware, etc.
3. Collection of related fields.
4. A group of records related by subject.
5. Person who develops computer system with users help, linking technology and user. (2 words)
6. Numbers, plus/minus signs and decimal points. (2 words, with 28 down)
7. It controls computing operation and functions. (2 words)
11. Screen that gives temporary output. (3 words, with 22 down)
14. Designs and writes own software. (2 words)
17. Software for production of pictures and diagrams.
18. ____ processing, allows input, editing etc. of textual data.
19. Handheld input device.
20. Group of related characters.
22. (last half of 11 down)
26. (chpt. 2) ____ code on/off bits that represent characters in computer memory.
28. (second half of 6 down)

CHAPTER 3

WORKSHEET: 3.1
PROJECT: 1

Name: _____

APPLICATION:

COMPONENT	INPUT	PROCESSING	OUTPUT	STORAGE
HARDWARE				
PROGRAMS				
DATA				
PROCEDURES				
PEOPLE				

WORKSHEET: 3.2
PROJECT: 3

Name:_____

	INPUT DESCRIPTION	INPUT TYPE	OUTPUT DESCRIPTION	OUTPUT TYPE
HOSPITAL PATIENT				
GROCERY BILL				
CAR IGNITION				
CONCERT TICKETS				
VIDEO GAME				

CHAPTER 3

WORKSHEET: 3.3
PROJECT: 4

Name:_____

SPECIFIC AREA:

IDEAS ON:
   DATA

   HARDWARE

   PROGRAMS

   PEOPLE

   PROCEDURES

HISTORICAL BACKGROUND:

FUTURE TRENDS:

CHAPTER 4: USING SOFTWARE

PURPOSE

This chapter surveys the types of systems and applications software available to users. Also, the process of translating and executing program instructions is reviewed.

TERMS TO REMEMBER

applications packages
assembler
command-driven operating system
compiler
communication software
computer-assisted design (CAD)
customized program
default
desktop publishing
execute
graphical user interface (GUI)
help screen
hypermedia
icon-driven operating system
independent software
integrated software
interactive
interpreter
linker

logic error
menu
multimedia
palette
promotional software
protected file
public domain software
robotics
scroll box
shareware
shell
supervisor
syntax error
tool box
terminate stay resident (TSR)
users' manual
utility software
window

ANSWERS TO REVIEW QUESTIONS

1. Define each "term to remember".

    applications packages -

    assembler -

    command-driven operating system -

compiler -

communication software -

computer-assisted design (CAD) -

customized program -

default -

desktop publishing -

execute -

graphical user interface (GUI) -

help screen -

hypermedia -

icon-driven operating system -

independent software -

integrated software -

interactive -

interpreter -

linker -

logic error -

menu -

multimedia -

palette -

promotional software -

protected file -

public domain software -

robotics -

scroll box -

shareware -

shell -

supervisor -

syntax error -

tool box -

Using Software

terminate stay resident (TSR) -

user's manual -

utility software -

window -

2. What are the functions of systems and applications software?

3. In what ways is properly designed software user-friendly?

4. What are two general types of applications software?
   1.
   2.

5. What four items are included as part of an applications package?

   1.

   2.

   3.

   4.

6. Describe the general characteristics of software that handles text processing, data management, graphics, multimedia presentations, and process control.

   text processing -

   data management -

   graphics -

   multimedia presentations -

   process control -

7. Identify eight questions users should ask when evaluating new software.

   1.

   2.

   3.

   4.

   5.

   6.

   7.

   8.

8. What is the critical difference between independent and integrated software?

9. How do windows, pull-down menus, icons, and help screens make applications software easier to use?

   Windows -

   Menus -

   Icons -

   Help screens -

10. Explain how a palette and tool box are used by a graphics package.

11. What type of information is found in a user's manual?

12. Identify and describe three types of systems software.

    1.

    2.

    3.

13. What are the two methods for booting an operating system into memory?

14. How are command-driven and icon-driven operating systems different?

15. Describe five responsibilities of an operating system.

    1.

    2.

    3.

    4.

    5.

16. How are assemblers different from high-level language translators?

17. Explain the differences between an interpreter and a compiler. Give an advantage and disadvantage to using each.

    interpreter -

    compiler -

18. What is the function of a linker program?

19. Identify eight jobs performed by utility software.

    1.
    2.
    3.
    4.
    5.
    6.
    7.
    8.

20. Identify five sources for computer software.

    1.
    2.
    3.
    4.
    5.

21. What is the advantage to purchasing software from a retail store?

22. What are three sources for public domain software?

   1.

   2.

   3.

23. How do you protect yourself from problems associated with public domain software?

24. How do users access information using hypermedia software?

PROJECTS

1. Write to a major manufacturer of software and see if promotional software or a low-cost tutorial is available for any of their packages. Note any copyright restrictions that may limit the number of copies that can be made.

2. A microcomputer can often use several different types of operating systems and graphical user interfaces (GUIs). Compare two different operating systems and/or GUIs by completing WORKSHEET 4.1.

3. Examine four application software packages available to users of your school computer lab or at a local computer store. For each list the package name, developer, cost, and three possible applications, if known. Use WORKSHEET 4.2 to complete this project.

4. Syntax errors can be avoided if the programmer is careful to follow the rules of a language. Using a manual for a high-level language available to you, make a list of the "vocabulary" of the language. Note any words that have a similar meaning in English.

5. Attend a local users' group meeting. Report on the conditions for membership, how often they meet, and the types of equipment on which they concentrate. Also see if the users' group is a source for shareware or public-domain software.

6. WHAT DO YOU THINK? Of the four major application packages talked about, which do you think will be most important to you in the future?

7. WHAT DO YOU THINK? Many young children are using computers. A key skill to effective computer use is the ability to touch-type. Do you think typing should be taught to all young computer users? At what age? Should typing be a pre-requisite for college and high school level computer classes? Why or why not?

WORKSHEETS

4.1 Comparison of operating systems

4.2 List of available application software

REFERENCES

Davis, William. *Operating Systems: A Systematic View* (3rd ed.). Reading, MA: Addison-Wesley Publishing Co., 1987.

Grantham, Tim. "Painting broad GUI landscape". *Canadian Datasystems*, April, 1991, pp. 18-20+.

Grauer, Robert T. and Paul K. Sugrue. *Microcomputer Applications*. New York: McGraw-Hill, 1987.

Grudin, Jonathan, "Interactive systems: Bridging the gaps between developers and users", *Computer*, April 1991, pp. 59-69.

Korzeniowski, Paul. "GUI tools still far from picture perfect". *Software*, April, 1991, pp. 90-92+.

Milenkovic, Milan. *Operating Systems: Concepts and Design*. New York: McGraw-Hill, 1987.

Rosenthal, Emily. *Hard Disk Software Management*. Portland, OR: Management Information Source, 1986.

Schneiderman, Ben, and Kearsley, Greg. *Hypertext Hands On! An Introduction to a New Way of Organizing and Accessing Information.* Reading, MA: Addison-Wesley, 1989.

The Software Catalog: Microcomputers. Netherlands: Elsevier Advanced Technology (reference service).

The Software Catalog: Minicomputers. Netherlands: Elsevier Advanced Technology (reference service).

Using Software

MIX AND MATCH

Match the following terms with the definitions below.
Each question has only one answer.

a. applications packages
b. assembler
c. command-driven
d. compiler
e. default
f. desktop publishing
g. execute
h. GUI
i. help screen
j. hypermedia
k. icon-driven
l. independent software
m. integrated software
n. interactive
o. interpreter
p. linker

q. logic error
r. menu
s. multimedia
t. palette
u. promotional software
v. robotics
w. scroll box
x. shareware
y. shell
z. supervisor
aa. syntax error
bb. tool box
cc. TSR
dd. user's manual
ee. utility software
ff. window

_____ 1. systems software doing common functions like sorting and file handling

_____ 2. software designed for personal productivity

_____ 3. changes operating system from command-driven to icon-driven

_____ 4. operating system requiring text as input

_____ 5. operating system program controlling all others

_____ 6. assumed instructions and formats

_____ 7. operating system requiring symbols as input

_____ 8. software that lets user control design and page layout of a text file

_____ 9. software that translates a program entirely before execution

_____ 10. when the computer follows program instructions

_____ 11. software supporting multimedia applications

_____ 12. software that translates simple abbreviations into machine code

_____ 13. spelling or punctuation error in programming

_____ 14. process control applications using robots

_____ 15. program that embeds utilities in translated code

_____ 16. software that translates and executes a program line by line

_____ 17. error that can be translated but gives wrong results

_____ 18. combination of text, sound, and graphic images

_____ 19. software unable to share data with other programs

_____ 20. list of program options available to a user

_____ 21. screen information to aid user

_____ 22. software able to share data with other programs

_____ 23. subdivided sections of a screen used to display output from several programs

_____ 24. direct communication with computer to answer requests

_____ 25. display of icons showing screen colors

_____ 26. written information on software or equipment

_____ 27. limited software to show a product's features

_____ 28. displays commands so user need not memorize them

_____ 29. display of icons showing drawing options

_____ 30. public domain software suggesting donations to authors for manual and revisions

_____ 31. program that is inactive but stays in computer's memory

_____ 32. displays lists or parts of graphs on small area of screen

Chapter 4

by A. Walters

ACROSS

1. ____ ____ operating system that works when user highlights icon representing a specific operation. (2 words)
2. Direct communication with computer where request is immediately acted on.
4. Programs that reside in the computer's memory, but stay inactive, until a special combination of keys are pressed. (3 words, with 3 down)
6. Following the program instructions one at a time.
8. ____ publishing, allows user precise control over page layout, typefaces, and graphic design.
9. Combination of text, numbers, sound, etc.
11. Standard assumptions computer follows, unless overridden by the user.
12. Displays color options in a graphics package.
14. Program modified for a specific application. (with 17 across)
17. (with 14 across)
18. Converts command-driven into icon-driven system. (abbr.)
20. Program in which people use computers to create two or three-dimensional drawings.
21. Area within a window. (2 words)
23. Software designed for user-oriented problems. (2 words)
25. ____ software, systems that perform jobs the operating system does not.
26. (2nd part of 17 down)
27. Information about application package. (2 words)

DOWN

1. ____ software, capable of using only data designated for it.
3. (with 4 across)
4. (chpt. 1) Another name for textual data.
5. Free-drawing graphic option containing drawing features.
7. Systems that work when user enters textual instructions. (2 words, with 15 down)
10. List of program options.
13. Software that translates programs into machine language. (pl.)
15. (2nd half of 7 down)
16. Display of operating instructions on command.
17. Program free to general public. (2 words, with 26 across)
19. ____ error, program error that is translatable but doesn't produce correct results.
20. High level language translator that checks entire program for errors while translating.
22. Use of robots for process control.
24. (chpt. 3) "Garbage in, garbage out."

CHAPTER 4

WORKSHEET: 4.1
PROJECT: 2

Name: _____

	OPERATING SYSTEM #1 OR GUI #1	OPERATING SYSTEM #1 OR GUI #1
MANUFACTURER		
BOOTED FROM DISK OR ROM		
MULTITASKING CAPABILITIES		
OPERATION	icon or command used to initiate action	icon or command used to initiate action
Display disk directory		
Display file on screen		
Print file		
Halt program execution		
Erase file		
Copy files		
Backup files		
Format new disk		
Check disk for bad sectors		
Change stored time and date		

Using Software

WORKSHEET: 4.2
PROJECT: 3

Name:_____

APPLICATION PACKAGE	APPLICATIONS
NAME: SOFTWARE DEVELOPER: COST:	1. 2. 3.
NAME: SOFTWARE DEVELOPER: COST:	1. 2. 3.
NAME: SOFTWARE DEVELOPER: COST:	1. 2. 3.
NAME: SOFTWARE DEVELOPER: COST:	1. 2. 3.

CLASS NOTES

CHAPTER 5: WORD PROCESSING AND DESKTOP PUBLISHING

PURPOSE

This chapter introduces the general commands and functions of a word processing and desktop publishing packages. Applications of word processing are discussed, along with the role of word processing in integrated software packages, and how to evaluate a word processing program. The chapter concludes with a discussion of good document designing features, applications for desktop publishing, and tips for selecting word processing software.

TERMS TO REMEMBER

block	import
boilerplate	landscape
clip art	office automation
cursor control	overwrite
discretionary replace	pagination
editing	pitch
electronic mail (E-mail)	point
electronic filing	portrait
electronic publishing	sans-serif
external copy	scroll
font	serif
footing	soft return
formatting	soft space
global replace	voice mail
hard return	white space
heading	word wrap
highlighting	WYSIWYG

ANSWERS TO REVIEW QUESTIONS

1. Define each "term to remember".

    block -

    boilerplate -

CHAPTER 5

clip art -

cursor control -

discretionary replace -

editing -

electronic mail (E-mail) -

electronic filing -

electronic publishing -

external copy -

font -

footing -

formatting -

global replace -

hard return -

heading -

highlighting -

import -

landscape -

office automation -

overwrite -

pagination -

pitch -

point -

portrait -

sans-serif -

scroll -

serif -

soft return -

soft space -

voice mail -

white space -

Word Processing and Desktop Publishing

word wrap -

WYSIWYG -

2. How do the following editing functions work?

word wrap -

cursor control -

insert -

delete -

move and copy -

search and replace -

save -

retrieve -

67

3. What are twelve formatting functions common to most word processing software?

   1.

   2.

   3.

   4.

   5.

   6.

   7.

   8.

   9.

   10.

   11.

   12.

4. How is a left justified document different from one with full or right justification?

5. Identify and describe six services that can be integrated with word processing software.

   1.

   2.

   3.

   4.

   5.

   6.

6. What formatting functions are controlled by style sheets?

   1.

   2.

   3.

   4.

   5.

   6.

   7.

7. When compared to word processing software, what additional levels of control are available with desktop publishing?

8. Explain six features of good document design and layout.

   1.

   2.

   3.

   4.

   5.

   6.

9. What sizes of type are associated with fine print, standard text, and headings or titles?

   fine print -

   standard text -

   headings or titles -

10. Identify situations when serif and sans-serif type is used.

11. Briefly describe the three basic file types desktop publishing software imports from other software packages.

    1.

    2.

    3.

12. Describe five functions of an automated office.

    1.

    2.

    3.

    4.

    5.

13. What is an advantage to sending mail electronically?

14. When is a paper copy necessary in a paperless office?

15. Explain how a business can use word processing software to create personalized advertising.

16. Describe eight ways the electronic office has changed journalism.

    1.

    2.

    3.

    4.

    5.

    6.

    7.

    8.

CHAPTER 5

17. What are five ways attorneys and legal secretaries utilize information technology in an automated office?

   1.

   2.

   3.

   4.

   5.

18. How do teachers and students use an electronic classroom?

19. How does automating offices facilitate the creation and distribution of new government legislation?

20. What seven steps should be a part of the evaluation process when purchasing a new word processing package?

   1.

   2.

   3.

   4.

   5.

   6.

   7.

Word Processing and Desktop Publishing

PROJECTS

1. Look at the manual and menus available on your word processing program. For the features listed in WORKSHEET 5.1, state the equivalent command or steps needed to produce the output described in the text.

2. On a one page "sampler" produce an example of the different fonts, pitches, and/or unique symbols available with your word processing package and/or desktop publishing package.

3. Design and type your resume using the word processor and/or desktop publisher. Many books are available in libraries containing sample formats for effective resumes.

4. As a follow-up to PROJECT #3, produce a sample cover letter to a prospective employer.

5. WHAT DO YOU THINK? Should word processing be available to students at all levels, even grade school? When would it be more important for students to produce handwritten documents rather than typed ones?

6. List five types of documents that could not be easily done on a word processor.

7. Desktop publishing is becoming very popular with small organizations. It allows them to do quality inhouse layout and production of brochures, advertising, etc. Investigate a desktop publishing package. Use WORKSHEET 5.2 to help you identify its features.

WORKSHEETS

5.1 Comparison of text terms with actual package commands

5.2 Desktop publishing package specifications

REFERENCES

All About Word Processing Systems. Delran, NJ: Data Pro Research, 1980- (information service).

Blair, Henry. "Users judge success of E-mail". *Information Management*, June, 1991, pp. 57-58+.

Datapro Reports of Office Automation. Delran, NJ: Data Pro Research, 1988- (information service).

Electronic Office. Pennsauken, NJ: Faulkner Technical Reports, 1988- (technical report).

Foley, Mary Jo. "PC word processing: The era of new and improved." *Datamation*, May 1, 1988, pp. 75-77.

Lagner, Mark. "Universal mailbox is E-mail goal". *Network World*, March 25, 1991, pp. 1+.

Mali, Paul and Richard W. Sykes. *Writing and Wordprocessing for Engineers and Scientists: How to Get Your Message Across in Today's High Technological World*. New York: McGraw-Hill, 1985.

Morgenstern, Steve. "Word Processing for Writers", *Home-Office Computing*, November, 1989, pp. 65-70.

Mullins, Carolyn J. "In another tongue [multilingual software]." *Information Center*, May 1988, pp. 38-41.

Panchak, Patricia L. "Selecting the right word processing software", *Modern Office*, May, 1991, pp. 85-86.

Rood, Fredrick T. "Cost-effective voice mail integration", *Voice Processing Magazine*, April, 1991, pp. 42+.

Trainor, Timothy and Stipes, Jeffrey. *Software Tools in Business: WordPerfect, Lotus 1-2-3, and dBase III Plus*. New York: Mitchell McGraw-Hill, 1991.

Word Processing and Desktop Publishing

MIX AND MATCH

Match the following terms with the definitions below.
Each question has only one answer.

a. block
b. boilerplate
c. clip art
d. cursor control
e. discretionary replace
f. editing
g. electronic mail
h. electronic filing
i. electronic publishing
j. external copy
k. font
l. footing
m. formatting
n. global replace
o. hard return
p. heading
q. highlighting

r. import
s. landscape
t. office automation
u. overwrite
v. pagination
w. pitch
x. point
y. portrait
z. sans-serif
aa. scroll
bb. serif
cc. soft return
dd. soft space
ee. voice mail
ff. white space
gg. word wrap
hh. WYSIWYG

_____ 1. blank spaces added between words in justification

_____ 2. networking office equipment to computers

_____ 3. computerized messaging system

_____ 4. maintaining files on computers instead of paper

_____ 5. carriage return generated by the user

_____ 6. inserted text replaces previous text

_____ 7. carriage return generated by the word wrap function

_____ 8. adding text or graphics created by another software package

_____ 9. short line segments added to type style for easier reading

_____ 10. feature that allows continuous input of text without carriage returns

_____ 11. function to move cursor up, down, left, right

_____ 12. moving page of text up, down, or side to side

75

_____ 13. system to record and maintain telephone calls on disk

_____ 14. section of text to be moved, copied, or deleted

_____ 15. changing intensity of blocks of text

_____ 16. horizontal page layout

_____ 17. area of document not filled with words or images

_____ 18. copying text from one file to another

_____ 19. partially completed document with areas left to be filled in later

_____ 20. computer automatically makes word substitution

_____ 21. user approves word substitution

_____ 22. functions to manipulate report's appearance

_____ 23. text appearing at top of each document page

_____ 24. text appearing at bottom of each document page

_____ 25. feature to control page numbering

_____ 26. feature that displays on the screen exactly what will be printed

_____ 27. type style weight and size of printed characters

_____ 28. number of characters printed per inch

_____ 29. technology to run high speed presses and control of document design

_____ 30. graphics purchased for use by designers

_____ 31. typeface measurement equal to 1/72nd of an inch

_____ 32. typeface lacking line segments resulting in block type

_____ 33. vertical page layout

_____ 34. controlling a document's final appearance

Chapter 5

by A. Walters

ACROSS

3. Lines of text that appear at the bottom of each document page.
5. Occurs when document is entered without carriage returns.
6. A carriage return entered into the text by the word-wrap function. (with 8 across)
8. (second half of 6 across)
9. Vertical page layout.
11. Selected text within a document that is deleted, moved, copied, or printed in a special format.
14. Increasing the intensity of characters on a screen for emphasis.
15. Copying a block or portion of a file to an outside file. (2 words)
20. The rolling of text up, down, and sideways on a screen for viewing long or wide documents.
22. Use of arrow keys to move cursor up, down, left, or right. (with 22 down)
23. (second half of 13 down)
26. To copy the text in memory onto disk.
28. ____ replace — each designated word is found and the user makes a decision whether to replace it or not.
29. ____ checker — misspellings are highlighted for correction.
30. Revising text.

DOWN

1. Style of printed character.
2. ____ drive — hardware that makes magnetic tape available for reading writing and storage (chpt. 3)
4. Lacking serifs which results in a simple, block style of printed text.
7. Controlling a document's final appearance.
8. Global ____ — automatic substitution of all occurrences of a word or phrase in a word processed document without user involvement.
10. Another name for textual data. (chpt. 1)
11. Partially completed document with space or codes for specific details that are added later.
12. Graphics and images on paper or disk that are purchased for use by designers. (2 words)
13. User can find synonyms for words in the text. (2 words, with 23 across)
16. Replacement of text by typing over the old text.
17. Adding graphics, image, or text created by other software to a document.
18. Horizontal page layout.
19. A carriage return entered into the text by the user.
21. To copy a text file on disk into memory.
22. (with 22 across)
24. Short line segment added to type style which helps eye flow across line of printed text.
25. Picture of items on a keyboard. (chpt. 1)
27. Unit of measure for type size equals 1/72nd of an inch.

CHAPTER 5

WORKSHEET: 5.1
PROJECT: 1   **Name:** _____

WORD PROCESSING PACKAGE:

FEATURE	ICON/COMMAND TO INTIATE ACTION
CURSOR CONTROL	
INSERT	
DELETE	
MOVE	
COPY	
RETRIEVE FILE	
SAVE FILE	
SEARCH AND REPLACE Global	
Discretionary	
SET LINE SPACING	
SET LEFT MARGIN	
SET RIGHT MARGIN	
SET HEADINGS	
SET FOOTINGS	
CENTER TEXT	
JUSTIFICATION Right Justified	
Ragged Right	

Word Processing and Desktop Publishing

WORKSHEET: 5.2
PROJECT: 4

Name: _____

DESKTOP PUBLISHING SOFTWARE:

PRICE:	SOFTWARE COMPANY
FEATURES	DESCRIPTION/REQUIREMENTS/LIMITS
COMPATIBLE OPERATING SYSTEM	
MINIMUM MEMORY REQUIREMENTS	
COMPATIBILITY WITH FILES FROM OTHER SOFTWARE	
INPUT/OUTPUT HARDWARE THAT CAN BE USED	
TEXT EDITING OPTIONS INSERT/CUT/COPY/DELETE	
USE OF GRAPHS, IMAGES INSERT/CUT/COPY	
PAGE LAYOUTS, STYLE SHEETS	
PRINT FONTS, PITCHES AVAILABLE	
SPECIAL FEATURES	
Margins & Columns	
Headings/Footings	
Titles, Bylines	
Vertical and Horizontal Lines	
Sizing & Scaling	
Other:	

CLASS NOTES

CHAPTER 6: ELECTRONIC SPREADSHEETS

PURPOSE

Electronic spreadsheets are examined in relation to their standard features, applications, and integration with other software packages. Also, tips on buying spreadsheet software are discussed.

TERMS TO REMEMBER

cell
command line
data entry line
fixed expenses
macro
range
status line
template
variable expenses
worksheet

ANSWERS TO REVIEW QUESTIONS

1. Define each "term to remember".

    cell -

    command line -

    data entry line -

    fixed expenses -

    macro -

    range -

status line -

template -

variable expenses -

worksheet -

2. What are two disadvantages to using paper-and-pencil worksheets?

   1.

   2.

3. What are two advantages to using electronic spreadsheets?

   1.

   2.

4. How are windows used with an electronic spreadsheet?

5. Explain the purpose of the data entry, format, move, copy, insert, remove, save, retrieve, print, protect, delete, and quit operations.

   data entry -

   format -

Electronic Spreadsheets

move -

copy -

insert -

remove -

save -

retrieve -

print -

protect -

delete -

quit -

6. What three types of values are used by an electronic spreadsheet?

   1.

   2.

   3.

7. Identify six advanced mathematical calculations performed by various spreadsheets.

   1.

   2.

   3.

   4.

   5.

   6.

8. Describe the advantages to integrating an electronic spreadsheet with databases, networks, and graphics programs.

9. What are the applications for electronic spreadsheets in school, at home, in sports, with volunteer organizations, as part of scientific analysis, and in manufacturing/design?

   Schools:

   Home:

   Sports:

Electronic Spreadsheets

Volunteer Activities:

Scientific Analysis:

Manufacturing/Design:

10. What five questions should you ask when evaluating electronic spreadsheet packages?

1.

2.

3.

4.

5.

PROJECTS

1. With guidelines given by your instructor, design and enter a simple spreadsheet concerning a budget or grade list. Make a hard copy after entering the initial data. Make the suggested changes to the data and print another copy.

2. Do a short paper (using a word processor, if possible) on the applications for spreadsheets in a particular field. Articles are available in professional journals. Or interview someone who uses a spreadsheet on the job. Find out how things were done before spreadsheets, how much time was involved, and what decision-making activities have been improved.

3. Use the manual and menus available for your spreadsheet to look up the features listed in WORKSHEET 6.1. State the equivalent command or steps needed to produce a similar action. This project dovetails nicely with APPLYING WHAT YOU'VE LEARNED question #4.

4. Do a side-by-side comparison of two spreadsheets, using the items listed in WORKSHEET 6.2. Information is available from user's manuals, sales literature, and computer stores.

5. WHAT DO YOU THINK? People working all day on computer equipment have higher incidence of these ailments: eyestrain, back pain, headaches, shoulder pain, etc. How do you a feel an organization can help these workers? Do you think that better designed equipment is the only answer? Should there be a maximum time a worker is allowed to use terminals each day?

WORKSHEETS

6.1 Comparison of text terms with actual package commands

6.2 Comparison of features on two spreadsheet packages

REFERENCES

Anderson, Kevin and Alan Bernard. "Spreading mistakes." *Journal of Accounting and EDP*, Winter 1988, pp. 42-45.

Berry, Tim. "The trouble with spreadsheets", *Personal Computing*, July, 1989, pp. 61- 63.

Berry, Tim. "How to structure spreadsheets." *Business Software*, October 1986, p. 56+.

Blodgett, Ralph. "Slashing time with macros", *Personal Computing*, July, 1989, pp. 53-54.

Hildebrand, Robert. "Playing what-if with a data table." *Lotus*, August 1986, pp. 56-61.

O'Leary, Timothy. *Microcomputing Lab Modules: Lotus 2.2*. New York: Mitchell McGraw-Hill, 1991.

O'Leary, Timothy. *Microcomputing Lab Modules: Quattro*. New York: Mitchell McGraw-Hill, 1991.

O'Leary, Timothy. *Microcomputing Lab Modules: SuperCalc 4.* New York: Mitchell McGraw-Hill, 1991.

Pitter, Keiko. *Using Application Software: Wordperfect, Quattro, dBase III Plus.* New York: McGraw-Hill, 1990.

Spreadsheet Disasters. Washington, D.C.: Hire Education, Inc., 1987.

Trainor, Timothy and Stipes, Jeffrey. *Software Tools in Business: WordPerfect, Lotus 1-2-3, and dBase III Plus.* New York: Mitchell McGraw-Hill, 1991.

MIX AND MATCH

Match the following terms with the definitions below.
Each question has only one answer.

a. cell
b. command line
c. data entry line
d. fixed expenses
e. macro
f. range
g. status line
h. template
i. variable expenses
j. worksheet

_____ 1. predictable, regular expenses

_____ 2. spreadsheet control line showing menu

_____ 3. intersection of spreadsheet row and column

_____ 4. spreadsheet control line showing input data

_____ 5. controllable expenses

_____ 6. spreadsheet control line showing current function

_____ 7. a predefined worksheet format with formulas but no data

_____ 8. small user-written program built into the spreadsheet to perform a combination of functions

_____ 9. manual organization of rows and columns of numbers

_____ 10. group of cells to be moved, copied, deleted, or affected by a formula

by A. Walters

ACROSS

1. Lets user change the worksheet's default settings.
4. Command that duplicates contents of a cell, row, or column to another location.
7. Location of spreadsheet function menus. (pl) (2 words)
10. Command to store a worksheet on a disk.
11. Software feature that allows the user to see parts of the worksheet that are not adjacent.
12. (chpt. 3) Handheld input device.
15. Area where initial input of spreadsheet data is stored. (3 words)
17. (second half of 14 down)
18. Bringing a worksheet from disk to screen.
19. Command to guard a file against being overwritten.
23. Command to place an empty row or column at a designated location.
24. Command to delete a row or column from a designated location.
25. They help organize financial records and perform mathematical functions.
26. (chpt. 1) Another name for textual data.

DOWN

2. A spreadsheet function which a user creates and retrieves with few keystrokes.
3. A worksheet with labels and formulas, formatted for a specific application where it is copied and reused.
4. Intersection of a worksheet row and column containing numbers, formulas, or text.
5. (chpt. 2) Work done while not connected to a computer.
6. Allows input of numbers, text and formulas onto a worksheet. (2 words)
8. Location reporting what operation is currently being performed. (2 words)
9. Regular, known expenses such as rent, and consumer loans. (2 words)
13. Operation that makes a hard copy of a worksheet.
14. Changeable expenses under consumer control. (2 words, with 17 across)
16. Command to erase a file from a disk.
20. A series of rows or columns identified by the first and last cells.
21. Command to leave the spreadsheet software and enter another package or operating system.
22. Command to allow changing of data from one position to another.

CHAPTER 6

WORKSHEET: 6.1
PROJECT: 3   Name:_____

SPREADSHEET PACKAGE:

FEATURE	ICON/COMMAND TO INITIATE ACTION
DATA ENTRY	
FORMAT	
MOVE	
COPY	
INSERT	
REMOVE	
SAVE	
RETRIEVE	
PRINT	
PROTECT	
DELETE	
QUIT	

Electronic Spreadsheets

WORKSHEET: 6.2
PROJECT: 4

Name:_____

	SPREADSHEET #1	SPREADSHEET #2
NAME		
SOFTWARE DEVELOPER		
COST		
COMPATIBLE OPERATING SYSTEMS		
MINIMUM MEMORY REQUIREMENTS		
MAXIMUM ROWS		
MAXIMUM COLUMNS		
NUMBER OF COMMANDS		
NUMBER OF MATHEMATICAL OPERATIONS		
NUMBER OF LOGICAL OPERATIONS		
COMPATIBLE SOFTWARE		

CLASS NOTES

CHAPTER 7: GRAPHICS

PURPOSE

Two basic types of graphics (presentation and free-drawing) are discussed in relation to a graphics package's features. Applications and buying tips for graphics programs are also examined.

TERMS TO REMEMBER

animation
bar graph
bit mapping
computer visualization
exploded pie chart
free drawing graphics
line graph
pie chart
presentation graphics
resolution
stacked bar graph

ANSWERS TO REVIEW QUESTIONS

1. Define each "term to remember".

    animation -

    bar graph -

    bit mapping -

    computer visualization -

    exploded pie chart -

CHAPTER 7

free-drawing graphics -

line graph -

pie chart -

presentation graphics -

resolution -

stacked bar graph -

2. What types of information are associated with each pixel in bit mapping?

3. Describe two ways to create a graphic image.

4. What are the four levels of information needed by graphics software to produce presentation graphics?

Graphics

5. What functions do the palette, toolbox, and pull-down menus provide for free-drawing graphics software?

   palette -

   tool box -

   pull-down menus -

6. How do the paintbrush, spraypaint, shapes, stretch, fill bucket, lasso, fatbits, eraser, and text options work?

   paintbrush -

   spraypaint -

   shapes -

   stretch -

   fill bucket -

   lasso -

   fatbits -

   eraser -

   text options -

CHAPTER 7

7. How do animators use computers in their work?

8. Identify ten free-drawing utilities that are available through pull-down menus.

   1.
   2.
   3.
   4.
   5.
   6.
   7.
   8.
   9.
   10.

9. How are computer-generated graphics used in computer-aided design, computer visualization, weather forecasting, space exploration, athletics and performing arts?

   computer-aided design:

   computer visualization:

   weather forecasting:

96

space exploration:

athletics:

performing arts:

10. What questions should you ask when selecting graphics software for personal use?

PROJECTS

1. Look at the free drawing graphics package available for your use. For the features listed in WORKSHEET 7.1, compare the terms in the text to the actual commands used in that specific package. The user manual accompanying the software package will help you with this.

2. Compare two graphics packages, using the points listed on WORKSHEET 7.2. Pick two packages that are similar in application; they can be for different machines.

3. Examine a presentation graphics package (or graphics part of an integrated software package) and report on its features. Include in the report:

   - what types of presentation graphics are available?
   - can data from other software be used in it?
   - what steps are required to enter data? identify labels? create titles? create legend?

4. Take a simple set of data and print it out in the three presentation graphics forms (pie chart, bar graph, and line chart). If a graphics package is not available, chart the data by hand on paper. In which form is the information clearest?

5. Make a sketch involving a free-drawing graphics package that uses as many options as possible. Print it out and label the options used.

6. WHAT DO YOU THINK? Do you think free-drawing graphics output should be considered art? Should it be displayed in museums, entered in art fairs, and for sale in galleries? Should it directly compete with more traditional forms of drawing -- or be considered an art form of its own? Would you pay for an "original" computer graphic?

7. WHAT DO YOU THINK? How do you think free-drawing computer graphics will affect the training and job of a landscape artist? a graphic artist? an animator?

WORKSHEETS

7.1 Comparison of text terms with actual package commands

7.2 Comparison of two similar graphics packages

REFERENCES

Aker, Sharon Z. *The Macintosh Bible Guide to SuperPaint.* New York: Goldstein and Blair, 1990.

Alperson, Jay R. and McComb, Gordon. *Designing, Producing, Using Business Graphics: With the Personal Computer.* Armonk, NY: IBM Armonk.

Goodman, Cynthia. *Digital Visions.* New York: Harry N. Abrams, 1987.

LoPiccolo, Phil. "The book of beasts", *Computer Graphics World*, April, 1991, pp. 94-96.

MacNicol, Gregory. "Rolling your own", *Computer Graphics World*, June, 1991, pp. 66-67+.

Magnenat-Thalmann, Nadia. *Computer Animation: Theory and Practice.* New York: Springer-Verlag, 1987.

Robertson, Barbara. "A painting revolution", *Computer Graphics World*, April, 1991, 34-37+.

Visual Computer: International Journal of Computer Graphics, The. Secaucus, NJ, 1989- (professional journal).

Weigner, Kathleen K. and Schlax, Julie. "What am I offered for this floppy disk?", *Forbes*, June 24, 1991, pp. 184-186+.

Wilson, Stephen. *Using Computers to Create Art.* Englewood Cliffs, NJ: Prentice-Hall, 1986.

CHAPTER 7

MIX AND MATCH

Match the following terms with the definitions below.
Each question has only one answer.

a. animation
b. bar graph
c. bit mapping
d. computer visualization
e. exploded pie chart
f. free-drawing graphics
g. line graph
h. pie chart
i. presentation graphics
j. resolution
k. stacked bar chart

_____ 1. presentation graphic showing data as parts of circle

_____ 2. another name for pixel graphics

_____ 3. graphics used for business applications

_____ 4. presentation graphics showing data as rectangles

_____ 5. graphics where computer is an artist's canvas

_____ 6. presentation graphic showing data as trends over time

_____ 7. bar chart containing several types of data on one bar

_____ 8. sequence of drawings showing motion

_____ 9. pie chart where pieces are separated from the circle

_____ 10. number of bits per line or inch in a drawing

_____ 11. computer-enhanced graphics that show images outside of human experience

Chapter 7

by A. Walters

ACROSS

1. ____ ____ graphics — using the computer to create drawings. (2 words)
5. Presentation graphic showing trends in data with one continuous line. (2 words)
6. To encircle an area of the graphic and that can then be moved, copied, or rotated.
8. Instrument with varying size and style options.
11. A pie chart where slices are separated from the main circle. (3 words)
12. Facts and figures. (chpt. 1)
13. (second part of 20 down)
15. An area of the graphic is chosen to be enlarged.
16. Menus brought down over the screen containing standard utilities to clear the screen. (2 words, with 18 across)
18. (second part of 16 across)
19. Another name for pixel graphics. (2 words)
21. As the cursor is moved around the screen a spattering of a chosen color or pattern is sprayed.
23. Picture representation of characters and figures other than those on your keyboard.
24. Groups of related characters. (pl) (chpt. 3)
25. A measure of graphic image sharpness in bits.

DOWN

1. Option to fill a shape with a chosen pattern or color.
2. When it is moved around the screen, the area beneath it is cleared.
3. The sequencing of motions produced by a series of drawn or generated frames.
4. Pattern of on/off bits used to represent characters or operations in computer memory. (chpt. 2)
7. Lets a user manipulate figures drawn with the shapes option.
9. Bar graphs where each bar is broken down to show its components. (pl) (3 words)
10. Allows users to choose the colors, shading, and pattern for the freehand drawing.
14. Contains a variety of options to let the user choose the type of drawing instrument and manipulate what is on the screen.
16. Business graphic showing wedges as pieces of the whole.
17. The user picks one of several common geometric figures, that are duplicated at a chosen location.
20. User may type text anywhere on the screen. (2 words, with 13 down)
22. Picture of an item on a keyboard. (chpt. 1)

WORKSHEET: 7.1
PROJECT: 1

Name: _____

GRAPHICS PACKAGE:

FEATURE	ICON/COMMAND TO INTIATE ACTION
PAINTBRUSH	
SPRAYPAINT	
SHAPES	
FILL BUCKET	
LASSO	
FATBITS	
ERASER	
TEXT	
CUT	
COPY	
PASTE	
QUIT	

Graphics

WORKSHEET: 7.2
PROJECT: 2   Name:_____

	GRAPHICS PACKAGE #1	GRAPHICS PACKAGE #2
NAME		
SOFTWARE		
COST		
COMPATIBLE OPERATING SYTEMS		
MINIMUM MEMORY REQUIREMENTS		
COLOR OR MONCHROME		
NUMBER OF DRAWING OPTIONS		
NUMBER OF FONTS		
SPECIAL INPUT HARDWARE		
SPECIAL OUTPUT HARDWARE		
COMPATIBLE SOFTWARE		

CLASS NOTES

CHAPTER 8: FILE AND DATABASE MANAGEMENT

PURPOSE

This chapter examines the different ways of organizing data into files or databases as well as methods for accessing these data resources.

TERMS TO REMEMBER

data administrator
data definition language
data manipulation language
data model
database management software
direct access
file management software
hashing routine
hierarchical model
indexed file
key field
natural language interpreter

network model
query
reference search
relational model
relative file
report writer
schema
sequential access
sequential file
subschema
table
updating

ANSWERS TO REVIEW QUESTIONS

1. Define each "term to remember".

    data administrator -

    data definition language -

    data manipulation language -

    data model -

CHAPTER 8

database management software -

direct access -

file management software -

hashing routine -

hierarchical model -

indexed file -

key field -

natural language interpreter -

network model -

query -

reference search -

relational model -

relative file -

report writer -

schema -

sequential access -

sequential file -

subschema -

table -

updating -

2. What are the five levels of data organization?

   1.

   2.

   3.

   4.

   5.

3. What is the difference between sequential and direct access? List the type of storage media used with each method.

4. How is a database management system different from a file management system?

5. Explain how a key field is used to access records from a sequential file, indexed file, and relative file.

   sequential file:

   indexed file:

   relative file:

File and Database Management

6. What are the advantages and disadvantages to using sequential, relative, and indexed files?

   sequential files

      advantages:

      disadvantages:

   indexed files

      advantages:

      disadvantage:

   relative files

      advantages:

      disadvantages:

7. What are two disadvantages to file processing?

   1.

   2.

8. Describe the important features of hierarchical, network, and relational database models.

   hierarchical model -

   network model -

relational model -

9. What are three responsibilities of a data administrator?

   1.

   2.

   3.

10. Explain the function of the Select, Append, Update, Sort, Index, Project, Join, and Subtract commands.

    Select command -

    Append command -

    Update command -

    Sort command -

    Index command -

    Project command -

    Join command -

    Subtract command -

File and Database Management

11. How is a database schema different from the data model?

12. What are three advantages to using a database and three potential disadvantages?

    Advantages

    1.

    2.

    3.

    Disadvantages

    1.

    2.

    3.

13. How do school administrators, teachers and counselors use file and database management?

14. In what ways can access to a database help doctors, pharmacists and public health officials?

CHAPTER 8

15. Explain how police officers, FBI agents, and judges utilize file and database management programs to perform their jobs.

16. What types of data are stored in a database used by farmers and livestock breeders?

17. How could the use of a reference search help you in school?

18. What questions should you answer before purchasing a data management package?

File and Database Management

PROJECTS

1. What file organization and access method would you suggest for the following applications? Use WORKSHEET 8.1 to complete this assignment.

   a) student information for college records
   b) vehicle registration file
   c) backing up a hard disk
   d) calculation of weekly payroll for a factory
   e) text and pictures for computer-based tutorials

2. Use WORKSHEET 8.2 to compare the general data manipulation language commands listed in the text with the actual commands used in a database at your disposal. What are the file and record limitations, along with memory requirements of the package?

3. Investigate the databases containing information related to your future career or another area of interest. Find out their names, rates of access, what kind of equipment is needed to access them, and other relevant information. Several reference sources exist that list online databases available throughout the country. See REFERENCES. Write up your findings in a short report.

4. WHAT DO YOU THINK? Some people in law enforcement and government advocate cross-referencing databases to help identify real or potential law breakers. For example: Cross social security numbers with draft registration to see who has not registered. Or compare names of government employees with lists of people who have defaulted on student loans for collection purposes. Do you think such uses of databases should be allowed? Can you name some applications that could be useful? Are there some applications potentially harmful to the privacy of individuals?

WORKSHEETS

8.1 Comparison of access methods and file organizations for five applications

8.2 Comparison of general and specific data manipulation language commands

REFERENCES

Adrion, W. Richard. "Information technology and the conduct of science", *Science*, February 12, 1988, pp. G67+.

Brogan Jim. "Data administration and the DBA", *Data Base*, February, 1991, pp. 18-20.

Data Processing Directory of On-Line Services. Delran, NJ: DataPro Research, 1982-.

Directory of Online Databases. Los Angeles, CA: Cuadra/Elsevier, 1985- (directory).

Mattison, Rob. "Selecting the right DBMS", *Data Base*, February 1991, pp. 29-30.

Radding, Alan. "Linking databases: Many paths", *Computerworld*, June 3, 1991, pp. 93-95.

Small, Jocelyn Penny. "Retrieving images verbally: No more key words and other heresies", *Library Hi Tech*, vol. 9, no. 1, pp. 51-60+.

Trainor, Timothy and Stipes, Jeffrey. *Software Tools in Business: WordPerfect, Lotus 1-2-3, and dBase III Plus*. New York: Mitchell McGraw-Hill, 1991.

Vacca, John R. "CASE and expert systems: Intelligent data bases", *Data Base*, May 1991, pp. 12-16.

File and Database Management

MIX AND MATCH

Match the following terms with the definitions below.
Each question has only one answer.

a. data administrator
b. data definition language
c. data manipulation language
d. data model
e. database management software
f. direct access
g. file management software
h. hashing routine
i. hierarchical model
j. indexed file
k. key field
l. natural language interpreter
m. network model
n. query
o. reference search
p. relational model
q. relative file
r. report writer
s. schema
t. sequential access
u. sequential file
v. subschema
w. table
x. updating

_____ 1. adding, deleting, or changing records

_____ 2. database model using top-down structure

_____ 3. retrieving data record-by-record

_____ 4. file where records are located by hashing routine

_____ 5. formula for converting key to disk location

_____ 6. field uniquely identifying a record

_____ 7. file with a directory for record look-up

_____ 8. database model with records accessible by several access paths

_____ 9. software for access to database information

_____ 10. system to manipulate simple files

_____ 11. plan that computer uses for storing and accessing data items

_____ 12. matrix (row-column) arrangement of relational data

_____ 13. file where data is in order by key field

_____ 14. language to set up a database

CHAPTER 8

_____ 15. person who establishes and evaluates a database record

_____ 16. database model using data tables

_____ 17. search through library databases for books using keywords

_____ 18. subset of defined relationships for a database

_____ 19. retrieving data in exact order needed

_____ 20. program allowing retrieval of database information with English commands

_____ 21. language to allow user to update database information

_____ 22. using a language to request database information

_____ 23. a logical plan of a database as viewed by people

_____ 24. database feature allowing users to set up document designs like headings and paging

Chapter 8

by A. Walters

ACROSS

1. Data ____ language. Series of commands that control the data base pgm.
4. A plan used by the computer for storing and accessing data. (2 words)
8. ____ management software. Computer program that maximizes access to one file at a time.
9. (second part of 2 down)
10. ____ file. Each record in the file is organized in sequence based on a key field.
11. ____ command. Reorganizes file into record order sequenced by key field identified by user.
12. Direct ____ — going directly to a record without reading any other records.
14. ____ command — allows a user to change data attributes in records.
16. ____ file — supports direct access to records in a file though a hashing routine that assigns each record to a specific disk loc.
18. ____ command — creates a smaller version of a data base file.
21. To look through a file or database to find references containing specific keywords. (2 words)
23. The schema for only the data included in a particular application.
24. Field within a record that uniquely identifies the record. (2 words)
25. Database model similar to a hierarchical mode but with additional pathways. (2 words)

DOWN

2. A data base pgm that translates English into computer-readable commands. (2 words, goes with 9 across)
3. ____ command — merges portions of multiple files into one file.
4. ____ language — commands used to identify fields and field characteristics in a data base record.
5. A database pgm that allows users to create hardcopy report formats for data output. (2 words)
6. ____ command — compares two files and creates a third containing data they do not have in common.
7. Database model where data is organized into tables, rows representing records while columns represent fields.
9. ____ file — supports direct access to records through the use of indexes.
11. ____ command — retrieves only the records and fields of user dictated criteria.
13. Command to store a worksheet on disk. (chpt. 6)
15. Data organized into rows and columns used in a relational database.
17. The organizational plan used to conceptualize a data base.
19. ____ command — used to set up the structure of the database by forming files and describing fields in records.
20. Handheld input device. (chpt. 3)
22. Intersection of a worksheet, row and column containing numbers, formulas or text. (chpt. 6)

CHAPTER 8

WORKSHEET: 8.1
PROJECT: 1   **Name:** _____

	FILE ORGANIZATION	ACCESS METHOD
STUDENT RECORDS		
VEHICLE REGISTRATION		
HARD DISK BACKUP		
PAYROLL RECORDS		
COMPUTER-BASED TUTORIAL		

File and Database Management

WORKSHEET: 8.2
PROJECT: 2

Name:_____

DATABASE PROGRAM:

REQUIREMENTS AND FEATURES	DESCRIPTION OF COMMANDS/ICONS AND REQUIREMENTS
SELECT	
APPEND	
UPDATE	
SORT	
INDEX	
PROJECT	
JOIN	
SUBTRACT	
MINIMUM MEMORY REQUIREMENTS	
MAXIMUM NUMBER OF FILES	
MAXIMUM NUMBER OF RECORDS/FILES	
MAXIMUM NUMBER OF FIELDS/RECORD	

CLASS NOTES

CHAPTER 9: PROCESSING HARDWARE

PURPOSE

The computer hardware is examined in two different perspectives within this chapter. The ways computer equipment can be configured to expand an organization's processing power are discussed. The chapter also looks at different processing hardware and how processing is done within them.

TERMS TO REMEMBER

address	megahertz (Mhz)
bus	MIPS
byte	motherboard
central processing unit (CPU)	multiprocessing
control character	primary storage
digital computer	random access memory (RAM)
distributed processing	read-only memory (ROM)
execution phase	real-time processing
expansion card	reduced instruction set computing (RISC)
expansion slot	secondary storage
fault-tolerant computer	teleprocessing
fetch phase	terabyte
gigabyte	terminal
kilobyte (K)	timesharing
machine code	virtual memory
megabyte (MB)	workstation

ANSWERS TO REVIEW QUESTIONS

1. Define each "term to remember".

    address -

    bus -

    byte -

    central processing unit (CPU) -

CHAPTER 9

control character -

digital computer -

distributed processing -

execution phase -

expansion card -

expansion slot -

fault-tolerant computer -

fetch phase -

gigabyte -

kilobyte (K) -

machine code -

megabyte (MB) -

megahertz (MHz) -

MIPS -

motherboard -

multiprocessing -

primary storage -

random access memory (RAM) -

read-only memory (ROM) -

real-time processing -

reduced instruction set computing (RISC) -

secondary storage -

teleprocessing -

terabyte -

terminal -

timesharing -

virtual memory -

workstation -

2. What are practical applications of real-time processing, teleprocessing, distributed processing, timesharing, and multiprocessing?

Real-time processing -

Teleprocessing -

Distributed processing -

Time-sharing -

Multiprocessing -

Processing Hardware

3. What are five characteristics for grouping processing hardware? Use these characteristics to differentiate among microcomputers, minicomputers, and mainframes.

   1.

   2.

   3.

   4.

   5.

4. Identify two types of portable microcomputers and explain how they are different from each other.

   1.

   2.

5. What are three applications for embedded computers and supercomputers?

6. How is a supercomputer different than a mainframe?

125

CHAPTER 9

7. Describe how fault-tolerant computers are different from other computers.

8. Describe how Boole's two-state mathematics is applied to computer-based instructions and data.

9. How are ASCII and EBCDIC used?

10. What are the two main parts of the central processing unit?

11. What is the difference between a millisecond, microsecond, nanosecond, and picosecond?

    millisecond -

    microsecond -

    nanosecond -

    picosecond -

12. Under what simple premise does the processor work?

13. Describe the operations performed by the processor.

14. What is stored in memory?

15. Describe the difference between volatile and non-volatile memory.

16. How are read-only memory and random access memory used?

17. Explain how the processor uses memory addresses to locate data and instructions.

18. How does virtual memory help to overcome the limits of memory?

19. How do the fetch and execution phases relate to IPOS?

20. What role does the computer's clock play in the CPU's processing cycles?

21. How are expansion cards used to add to a microcomputer's capabilities?

22. How much time and what tools are needed for building a personal computer?

PROJECTS

1. Complete the chart on WORKSHEET 9.1 comparing real-time, processing, teleprocessing, multitasking, multiprocessing, and distributed processing. For each, list the number and types (mainframe, mini, micro) of computers involved, what kinds (if any) of peripherals are needed, and applications where this type of processing is necessary.

2. Investigate an organization that uses a mainframe computer, supercomputer, or a fault-tolerant computer. What conditions exist that make this type of processing necessary? How did the organization cope before this equipment was available? What are the features of this machine? Memory? Speed? Peripherals? Is it owned or leased? What type of processing applications (real-time, distributed processing, etc.) are involved?

Processing Hardware

3. Use WORKSHEET 9.2 to compare the specifications of a microcomputer, minicomputer, and mainframe. Pick one model for each size of computer. Possible resources for this information are local computer stores, manufacturers, organizations using the equipment, and magazine advertisements.

4. Complete WORKSHEET 9.3 to examine a microcomputer available to you on-campus, at home, or at work. Use the information and terms acquired in this chapter as well as from Chapter 1 and 3.

5. WHAT DO YOU THINK? Should customers be able to sue computer manufacturers or software developers when programs or equipment do not work correctly? Would it make a difference if the problems caused a business or customer to lose money? Damage property? Cause injury to another person?

WORKSHEETS

9.1 Comparison of processing options

9.2 Comparison of computers by size, speed, cost, and memory

9.3 Analysis of microcomputer features

REFERENCES

Coffman, Cathy and Yeich, Christopher. "RISCy business", *Automotive Industries*, February 1991, pp. 133-137.

Ebert, Jon. "Managing change in a distributed environment", *Enterprise Systems Journal*, May, 1991, pp. 56+.

Horwitt, Elisabeth. "Distributing computing arises", *Computerworld*, April 15, 1991, pp. 49+.

Minicomputers. Pennsauken, NJ: Faulkner Technical Reports, 1988- (technical report).

Seybold, Andrew M. "The true costs of portable computing", *Computerworld*, June 24, 1991, p. 84.

Therrien, Lois and Buel, Barbara. "Whatever happened to the corner computer store?" *Business Week*, May 20, 1991, pp. 131-132+.

CHAPTER 9

MIX AND MATCH

Match the following terms with the definitions below.
Each question has only one answer.

a. address
b. bus
c. byte
d. CPU
e. control character
f. digital computer
g. distributed processing
h. execution phase
i. expansion card
j. expansion slot
k. fault-tolerant
l. fetch cycle
m. gigabyte
n. kilobyte (K)
o. machine code
p. megabyte (MB)
q. megahertz (MHz)
r. MIPS
s. motherboard
t. multiprocessing
u. primary storage
v. random access memory (RAM)
w. read-only memory (ROM)
x. real-time processing
y. RISC
z. secondary storage
aa. teleprocessing
bb. terabyte
cc. terminal
dd. timesharing
ee. virtual memory
ff. workstation

_____ 1. processing where results are immediately available

_____ 2. one million bytes

_____ 3. communication lines connect remote components

_____ 4. type of volatile memory containing programs and data

_____ 5. device at end of a communication line

_____ 6. place in microcomputer where additional memory may be added

_____ 7. one billion bytes

_____ 8. binary code used to represent program instructions

_____ 9. processor with few instruction codes

_____ 10. measurement of processing speed in mainframe computer

_____ 11. teleprocessing system with more than one computer

_____ 12. many users sharing the the power of a single computer

Processing Hardware

_____ 13. processing phase where instruction and data are retrieved from memory

_____ 14. simultaneous execution an application by several computers

_____ 15. computer designed to never crash

_____ 16. computers using data expressed as electronic impulses

_____ 17. a bit pattern representing a single character or program instruction

_____ 18. one thousand bytes

_____ 19. part of computer containing memory and processor

_____ 20. microcomputer used as a terminal for a mainframe

_____ 21. another name for memory

_____ 22. circuitry connecting CPU with external and internal hardware

_____ 23. one trillion bytes

_____ 24. hardware to store data; like disks and tape

_____ 25. type of non-volatile memory containing systems program

_____ 26. measurement of processing speed in microcomputers

_____ 27. expansion of primary storage onto disk

_____ 28. number which identifies storage locations in memory

_____ 29. special symbols representing cursor movement, tabs, etc.

_____ 30. central area where the RAM, ROM, and other processing circuitry reside in a microcomputer

_____ 31. processing phase where arithmetic/logic is performed

_____ 32. additional processing power that can be plugged into a microcomputer

Chapter 9

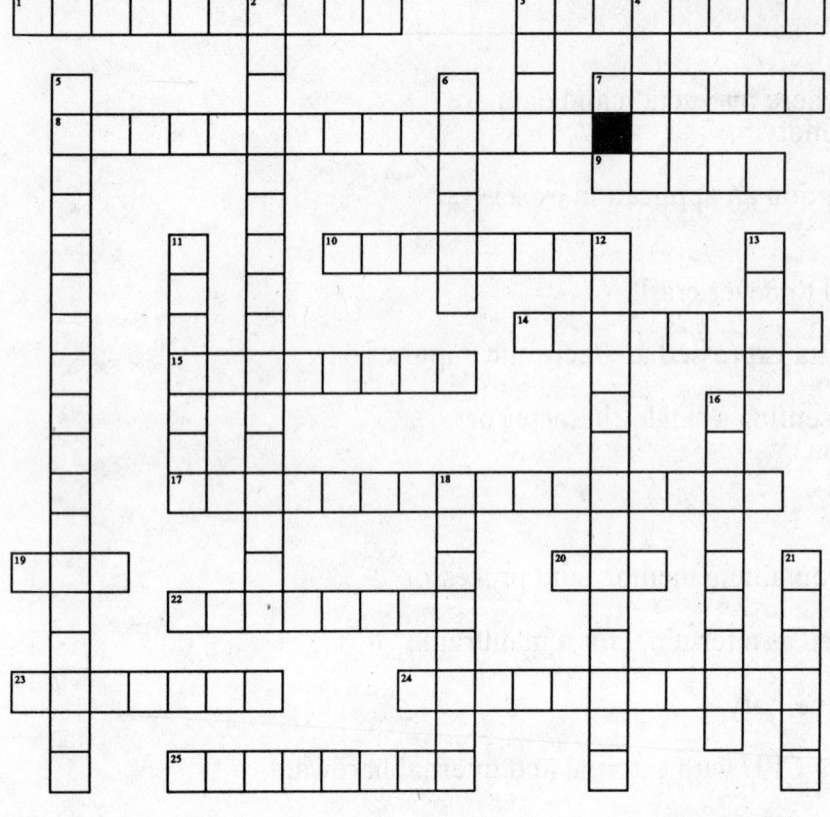

by A. Walters

ACROSS

1. One billionth of a second; used to measure computer speed within the processor.
3. One million bytes of memory.
7. (chpt. 5) Rolling of text up, down, and sideways on a screen for viewing longer wider documents.
8. Part of processing cycle where arithmetic or logic operation is performed by processor and results are sent to memory.
9. (chpt. 4) Group of related characters.
10. Fault-____ computer. A computer with duplicate processing components that are designed to switch to one set when the other set has problems.
14. Approximately 1,000 bytes of memory.
15. ____ ____ memory. Permanent memory, programmed during manufacturing, which holds systems programs and language translators. (2 words)
17. ____ ____ another name for storage on disks or tapes. (2 words)
19. Path (circuitry) that connects the CPU with internal and external hardware.
20. (third word of 5 down)
22. I/O device at end of communication line where message terminates.
23. ____ computer that accepts programs and data as binary code.
24. ____ processing system contains more than one computer to decentralize processing.
25. One trillion bytes of memory.

DOWN

2. Special instruction like carriage return cursor movement, etc. (2 words)
3. Million instructions per second; a measurement of processing speed on computers.
4. Binary code for storing data that uses seven bits to a byte and is commonly used in microcomputers. (abbr.)
5. ____ ____ ____ computing. Processor designed to achieve faster processing speeds by minimizing intermediary processing steps through limiting the number of complex operations. (3 words, with 20 across)
6. (chpt. 7) User picks one of several geometric figures that are duplicated at a chosen location.
11. Unique number assigned to each memory location within a computer.
12. Information is transferred between a computer and terminals at remote locations by using communications lines.
13. A group of bits representing a single character of data.
16. Million cycles per second; a measurement of a microprocessor's processing speed.
18. ____ ____ processing. When the computer system returns results as soon as processing is done. (2 words)
21. Binary code for storing data that uses eight bits per byte and is used in minicomputers and mainframes. (abbr.)

Processing Hardware

WORKSHEET: 9.1
PROJECT: 1

Name:_____

	COMPUTERS	PERIHERALS	APPPLICATIONS
REAL-TIME PROCESSING			
TELEPROCESSING			
DISTRIBUTED PROCESSING			
MULTI-TASKING			
MULTI-PROCESSING			

WORKSHEET: 9.2
PROJECT: 3

Name:_____

	MICROCOMPUTER	MINICOMPUTER	MAINFRAME
MANUFACTURER & MODEL			
PHYSICAL DEMENSIONS			
MEMORY Maximum & Minimum Bytes			
SPEED Instructions per second			
COST			

Processing Hardware

WORKSHEET: 9.3
PROJECT: 4

Name:_____

MANUFACTURER/MODEL:

PHYSICAL DIMENSIONS	PRICE
MEMORY: RAM	ROM
OPERATING SYSTEM	BOOTED FROM ROM OR DISK?
KEYBOARD: Cursor Control	Function Keys
Numeric Keypad	Detachable
SCREEN: Dimensions	Color
	Graphics
STORAGE: DRIVE #1 Type Capacity	DRIVE #2 (optional) Type Capacity Additional Cost
ADDITIONAL INPUT HARDWARE Description Price	ADDITIONAL OUTPUT HARDWARE Description Price

CLASS NOTES

CHAPTER 10: PERIPHERALS

PURPOSE

This chapter shows how a variety of input, output, and storage hardware can be used to tailor a computer system to a specific user problem. The types of data and input handled by the hardware, as well as relevant procedures for I/O, are discussed.

TERMS TO REMEMBER

bar codes
blocks
buffer
computer output microfilm (COM)
correspondence quality character
CRT (cathode ray tube)
cylinder
digitize
disk directories
disk track
diskette
dot-matrix character
draft-quality printer
dumb terminal
floppy disk
formatting
full character
function key
hard copy
hard-copy terminal
hard disk
hard-sectored diskette
head crash
intelligent terminal
I/O (Input/Output)
joystick
letter-quality printer
light pen
line printer
liquid crystal display (LCD)
monitor
monochrome
numerical control (NC)
optical disk
page printer
parallel port
parity bit
parity checking
plotter
point-of-sale (POS)
remote job entry
RGB (Red, Green, Blue) monitor
scanner
sector
serial port
serial printer
soft copy
soft-sectored diskette
tablet
tape streamer
tape tracks
touch-sensitive screen
voice recognition device

ANSWERS TO REVIEW QUESTIONS

1. Define each "term to remember".

   bar codes -

   blocks -

   buffer -

   computer output microfilm (COM) -

   correspondence quality character -

   CRT (cathode ray tube) -

   cylinder -

   digitize -

   disk directories -

   disk track -

   diskette -

Peripherals

dot-matrix character -

draft-quality printer -

dumb terminal -

floppy disk -

formatting -

full character -

function key -

hard copy -

hard-copy terminal -

hard disk -

hard-sectored diskette -

head crash -

intelligent terminal -

I/O (Input/Output) -

joystick -

letter-quality printer -

light pen -

line printer -

liquid crystal display (LCD) -

monitor -

monochrome -

numerical control (NC) -

optical disk -

page printer -

Peripherals

parallel port -

parity bit -

parity checking -

plotter -

point-of-sale (POS) -

remote job entry -

RGB (Red, Green, Blue) monitor -

scanner -

sector -

serial port -

serial printer -

soft copy -

soft-sectored diskette -

tablet -

tape streamer -

tape tracks -

touch-sensitive screen -

voice recognition -

2. Describe the difference between interactive and batch input.

3. What are the advantages and disadvantages to using dumb and intelligent terminals?

Peripherals

4. Define four types of machine-readable data read by scanners and describe an application for each.

   1.

   2.

   3.

   4.

5. How can a telephone and card reader be used as part of input operations?

6. Describe an application for voice recognition devices and identify three limitations to using this equipment.

7. How is a sensor used as an input peripheral?

8. What are the different speeds of serial, line and page printers?

9. How do ink-jet, thermal, electrostatic, and laser printers work?

   Ink-jet printers -

   Thermal printers -

   Electrostatic printers -

   Laser printers -

10. What are the advantages and disadvantages to using a plotter for output?

11. Why would an organization use Computer Output Microfilm (COM)?

12. Describe two ways of storing reduced images by using COM.

    1.

    2.

13. Name and describe the differences in the four standards for color monitors.

    1.

    2.

    3.

    4.

Peripherals

14. Describe an application for sound synthesizers and speech synthesizers.

15. What determines the movement (output) of a robot?

16. What are the three types of tape storage?

    1.

    2.

    3.

17. Explain how parity checking works when reading a nine-track tape.

18. What is the purpose of interrecord and interblock gaps?

19. Why are records often grouped into blocks when recorded on tape?

145

20. How are header and trailer labels used in file processing?

21. What are the two most common types of magnetic disk storage?

    1.

    2.

22. How is data stored in disks?

23. What are four distinguishing features of a floppy disk?

    1.

    2.

    3.

    4.

24. Describe what happens when a disk is formatted.

25. How is the disk directory used to locate files or programs on disk?

26. Give and advantage and disadvantage to using disk drives with removable and fixed disks.

27. Describe the difference between access time and transfer rate.

28. Explain how optical disks work, and identify one advantage and disadvantage to using this technology.

29. How does mass storage work? What types of organizations would benefit from mass storage?

PROJECTS

1. What storage hardware would you suggest for the following applications? These applications were previously investigated in Project #1 in Chapter 8.

    a) student information for college records
    b) vehicle registration file
    c) backing up a hard disk
    d) calculation of weekly payroll for a factory
    e) text and pictures for computer-based tutorials

2. Many types of storage media are available for use on microcomputers. Go to a computer store or look through a computer magazine to find at least three different storage media. Use WORKSHEET 10.1 to organize information on their storage capacity, access speed, price, and any other distinguishing characteristics.

3. Name three possible applications for sound and speech output other than those mentioned in the text.

4. Assume you are buying a printer for your home, computer lab (or a special application). By visiting a computer store or reading ads in magazines, compare two printers on size, price, speed, and other qualities mentioned in the text. Which would you buy? Use WORKSHEET 10.2 to aid in your investigation.

5. Given the list of input/output hardware shown on WORKSHEET 10.3 fill in what types of problems they could help solve.

6. WHAT DO YOU THINK? Some people feel that computers contribute to the "dehumanization" of many activities such as buying products, applying for loans, keeping bank accounts. They complain that we are no longer people but numbers and that personal service is on the decline. Do you think this is true? Can an organization, like a bank or store, use the technology yet still capture that "neighborhood" feeling? How?

WORKSHEETS

10.1 Fact sheet on the tape or disk drives available at the college

10.2 Printer comparison sheet

10.3 Problem solving with the help of I/O hardware

REFERENCES

Ainsbury, Robert. *Using your Hard Disk.* Carmel, IN: Que Corporation, 1990.

Anderson, Robert. "A case for not so dumb terminals", *Information Management*, April, 1991, pp. 69-71.

Berliner, Don. *Managing your Hard Disk.* Carmel, IN: Que Corporation, 1988.

Bond, John. "Printers show their colors as performance and reliability improve." *Computer Decisions*, January 1988, pp. 43-44+.

Byers, T. J. "How to add a hard disk", *PC World*, May, 1991, pp. 203-207.

Crawford, Walt. "Catching pictures, catching words: Low-cost scanning and optical character recognition". *Library Hi Tech*, vol, 9, no. 1, pp. 91-112.

Honan, Patrick. "Bigger! Faster! Cheaper! New storage technologies boost speed and capacity, cut costs", *Lotus*, March 1991, pp. 63-66.

Johnson, Laura K. "A cheaper way to print", *Datamation*, May 1, 1991, pp. 75-77.

Meyer, Frederick P. "Information management: An overview of CD-ROM technology", *Data Resource Management*, Spring, 1991, pp. 14-19.

Normile, Dennis and Johnson, J. T. "Computers without keys", *Popular Science*, August, 1990, pp. 66-69.

Patsch, Glenn R. "All about floppy disks", *Electronic Servicing and Technology*, August, 1990, pp. 37+.

Putman, Byron W. *RS232 Simplified: Everything You Need To Know about Connections, Interfaces, and Troubleshooting Peripheral Devices.* Englewood Cliffs, NJ: Prentice-Hall, 1987.

Richter, Jake. "XGA: a new graphics standard", *Byte*, February, 1991, pp. 285-290.

Shneiderman, Ben. "Touch screens now offer compelling uses", *IEEE Software*, March, 1991, pp. 93-94+.

Williams, R. R. and Shellman, R. L. "Smart data acquisition: Coupling microcontrollers and sensors". *Scientific Computing and Automation*, February 1989, pp.59-62.

Yakal, Kathy. "Optical disk hardware: A mix of alternatives", *The Office*, April, 1991, pp. 8+.

CHAPTER 10

MIX AND MATCH

Match the following terms with the definitions below.
Each question has only one answer.

a. bar codes
b. blocks
c. buffer
d. COM
e. correspondence quality character
f. CRT
g. cylinder
h. digitize
i. disk directory
j. disk track
k. diskette
l. dot-matrix character
m. draft-quality printer
n. dumb terminal
o. floppy disk
p. formatting
q. full character
r. function key
s. hard copy
t. hard-copy terminal
u. hard disk
v. hard-sectored diskette
w. head crash
x. intelligent terminal
y. I/O
z. joystick
aa. letter-quality printer

bb. light pen
cc. line printer
dd. LCD
ee. monitor
ff. monochrome
gg. numerical control (NC)
hh. optical disk
ii. page printer
jj. parallel port
kk. parity bit
ll. parity checking
mm. plotter
nn. point-of-sale (POS)
oo. remote job entry
pp. RGB monitor
qq. scanner
rr. sector
ss. serial port
tt. serial printer
uu. soft copy
vv. soft-sectored diskette
ww. tablet
xx. tape streamer
yy. tape tracks
zz. touch-sensitive screen
aaa. voice recognition device

_____ 1. operations where data is entered and results received from a computer

_____ 2. sending data from geographically different areas through communications lines for centralized processing

_____ 3. data displayed on a VDT screen

_____ 4. paper copy of output

_____ 5. terminals producing paper copies of output

_____ 6. terminals with no built-in processing power

150

Peripherals

_____ 7. terminals with built-in memory and processing power

_____ 8. keys that initiate special software features

_____ 9. hand-held input device looking like a stylus

_____ 10. screen allowing data input through direct contact

_____ 11. flat pressure-sensitive surface used for drawing

_____ 12. method for screen display on portable computers

_____ 13. input hardware accepting spoken commands

_____ 14. I/O port handling one byte at a time

_____ 15. data found on grocery products

_____ 16. hardware to read OCR, OMR, and bar codes

_____ 17. printed characters made up of dots

_____ 18. printer using dot-matrix characters

_____ 19. characters overprinted for clarity

_____ 20. preformed printed characters

_____ 21. printer using full characters

_____ 22. printer producing one character at a time

_____ 23. printer producing one line at a time

_____ 24. printer producing one page at a time

_____ 25. hardware producing graphics on paper

_____ 26. I/O port handling one bit at a time

_____ 27. techniques to transfer output onto microfilm or microfiche

_____ 28. another name for VDT

_____ 29. screens producing single color output

_____ 30. screens producing color output

_____ 31. machines using numerical specifications to produce precision parts

_____ 32. input device moved around like a car's stick shift

_____ 33. input of sales data at the location of the sale

_____ 34. bit used to check accuracy of input data

_____ 35. channels holding bits on tape

_____ 36. error checking using a bit to maintain an even or odd number of "on" bits

_____ 37. portion of memory used for temporary data storage

_____ 38. disk with inflexible platters

_____ 39. collection of records read or written at one time

_____ 40. small flexible disks, also called diskettes

_____ 41. concentric circles on disks containing data

_____ 42. subdivision of disk track

_____ 43. diskette with a series of sensing holes

_____ 44. list of file header label locations on a diskette

_____ 45. to set up tracks and sectors on a diskette

_____ 46. diskette where sectors are identified by a series of sensing holes

_____ 47. disk tracks read by one positioning of the access arm

_____ 48. high-speed media read by lasers

_____ 49. read/write head actually touches disk surface

_____ 50. another name for VDT

_____ 51. another name for floppy disk

_____ 52. to convert location of input device into mathematical terms

_____ 53. form of magnetic tape used for backup

Chapter 10

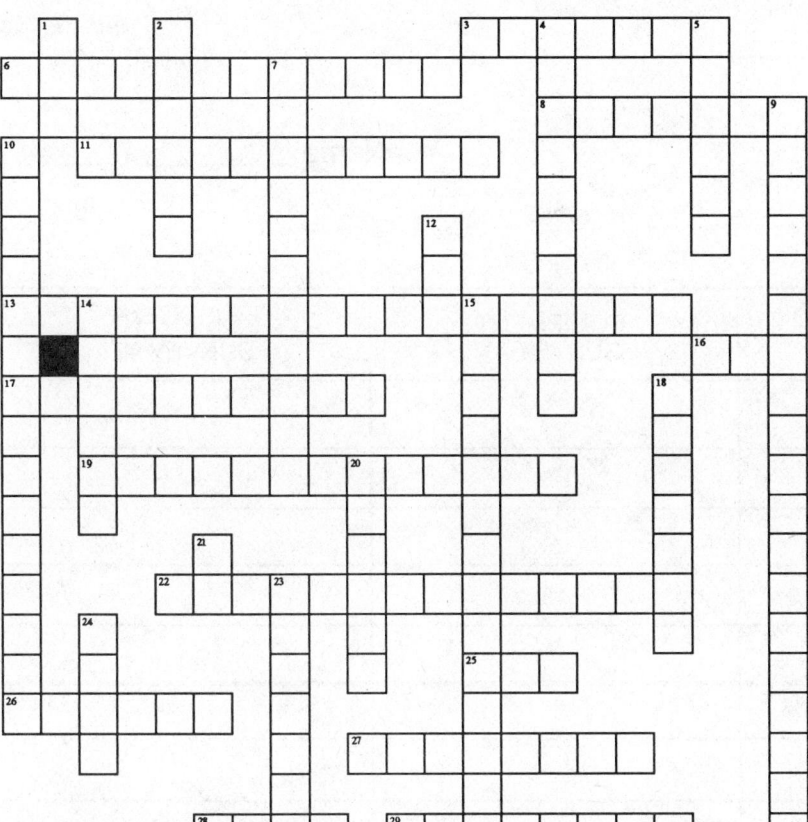

by A. Walters

ACROSS

3. System of machine readable input that allows scanners to read pencil marks used on standardized tests and surveys. (first word with 28 across and 11 across)

6. A record that marks the end of a file on tape and disk. (2 words)

8. Page ____. Produces one page of output at a time with speeds to 6 to 20,000 lines per minute.

11. (3rd word with 3 across and 28 across)

13. A type of character made up of dots. (3 words)

16. Color monitor standard that displays 720 x 400 in 256 colors. (abbr.)

17. Multicolor monitor using red, green, and blue pixels to form a variety of colors. (abbr., 2 words)

19. ____ printers. Used electrical impulses to put characters on electrostatic paper.

22. ____ ____ microfile. Microfiche of data by a computer. (2 words)

25. Color monitor standard that displays 720 x 350 pixels in 16 colors. (abbr.)

26. I/O port sending data one bit at a time. (2 words, with 24 down)

27. Data displayed on a monitor. (2 words)

28. (second word with 1 across and 11 across)

29. Lever moved around like an automobile stick shift, its action moving a cursor or object on the monitor.

DOWN

1. Another name for a monitor. (abbr.)

2. Groups of records on a tape organized for more efficient I/O.

4. The eight or nine channels where data is written as bits on tape. (2 words)

5. ____ ____ printer uses full characters. (2 words, with 18 down)

7. Printer producing a line at a time (100 to 2000 lines per minute). (2 words)

9. A drive that can use more than one disk but has slower access time than fixed disk drives. (3 words)

10. Listings of the locations of the header labels for all files on several disks.

12. Color monitor that displays 1024 x 786 pixels in 536 colors. (abbr.)

14. Sensitized table on which the position of a special pen is used as data.

15. Sending data in a batch from remote area to central mainframe. (3 words)

18. (second word of 5 down)

20. A division of a disk track used to locate data.

21. Operations where people use peripherals to send data and receive information. (abbr.)

23. An output device that produces line drawings by moving a pen across paper.

24. (2nd part with 26 across)

WORKSHEET: 10.1
PROJECT: 2

Name:_____

	EQUIPMENT SURVEY #1	EQUIPMENT SURVEY #2
TAPE:		
MANUFACTURER/MODEL		
BYTES STORED/INCH		
ACCESS SPEED		
COST		
FLOPPY DISK:		
MANUFACTURER/MODEL		
HARD/SOFT SECTOR		
NO. TRACKS		
NO. BYTES STORED		
ACCESS SPEED		
DISK COST		
DRIVE COST		
HARD DISK:		
MANUFACTURER/MODEL		
NO. PLATTERS		
NO. TRACKS/PLATTER		
NO. BYTES STORED		
ACCESS SPEED		
DISK COST		
DRIVE COST		

Peripherals

WORKSHEET: 10.2
PROJECT: 4

Name: _____

	PRINTER #1	PRINTER #2
MANUFACTURER AND MODEL		
PRINT IMAGE (Dot Matrix or Full Character)		
PRINTING SPEED		
MAXIMUM PAPER WIDTH		
TYPE STYLE		
GRAPHICS		
SINGLE PAPER FEED		
OTHER OPTIONS		
DIMENSIONS		
PRICE		

CHAPTER 10

WORKSHEET: 10.3
PROJECT: 5

Name: _____

I/O HARDWARE	PROBLEM/SOLUTION
MOUSE	
INTELLIGENT TERMINAL	
LIGHT PEN	
JOYSTICK	
SCANNER	
BAR CODE	
VOICE RECOGNITION	
VOICE SYNTHESIZER	
SOUND SYNTHESIZER	
PLOTTER	
COMPUTER OUTPUT MICROFILM	
ROBOT OR OTHER ACTION HARDWARE	

CHAPTER 11: DATA COMMUNICATIONS

PURPOSE

The technology concerning distributed processing and networks is examined in this chapter. Analysis includes communications software and hardware, network topologies, and problems data communications can help solve.

TERMS TO REMEMBER

acoustic coupler
analog signals
asynchronous
baud rate
bits per second (bps)
bus topology
communication channel
concentrator
data communication
digital signals
direct-connect modem
download
electronic bulletin board system (BBS)
electronic funds transfer (EFT)
facsimile (fax) machine
file server
gateway
hardwired
host

hybrid topology
information utility
local area network (LAN)
modem
multiplexer
network
network topology
node
ring topology
smart card
smart modem
star topology
synchronous
telecommunication
telecommuting
teleconferencing
upload
value-added network (VAN)
wide area network (WAN)

ANSWERS TO REVIEW QUESTIONS

1. Define each "term to remember."

    acoustic coupler -

    analog signals -

    asynchronous -

baud rate -

bits per second (bps) -

bus topology -

communication channel -

concentrator -

data communication -

digital signals -

direct-connect modem -

download -

electronic bulletin board system (BBS) -

electronic funds transfer (EFT) -

facsimile (fax) machine -

file server -

gateway -

hardwired -

host -

hybrid topology -

information utility -

local area network (LAN) -

modem -

multiplexer -

network -

network topology -

node -

CHAPTER 11

ring topology -

smart card -

smart modem -

star topology -

synchronous -

telecommunication -

telecommuting -

teleconferencing -

upload -

· value-added network (VAN) -

wide area network (WAN) -

Data Communications

2. How do simplex, half-duplex, and full-duplex transmission work?

   simplex -

   half-duplex -

   full-duplex -

3. When is it best to use bps versus baud rate?

4. Why are modems needed for data communications?

5. What are the two different types of direct-connect modems?
   1.
   2.

6. Name the advantages and disadvantages of using a fax machine.

7. Name four types of communication channels and identify the transmission speeds associated with each.
   1.
   2.
   3.
   4.

CHAPTER 11

8. What are the responsibilities of a bulletin board's sysop?

9. Describe how people would use an electronic bulletin board system and information utilities.

10. What is the difference between electronic mail, voice mail, and electronic data interchange?

11. How does electronic funds transfer work?

12. What features and options should you look for in communication software?

Data Communications

PROJECTS

1. Take one of the network topology figures in the text and redraw it to reflect a network in a organization nearby. The network could be situated in the college, at work, at a franchise store you frequent, or a government office, for example. Label the location of each computer and the type of communication lines, if known.

2. Investigate the cost and specifications for a modem to connect a school or home microcomputer with the college's main computer. Use WORKSHEET 11.1 to help you. Information can be obtained from the college computer center, magazines, and local computer stores.

3. Contact the local computer users' group to see what electronic bulletin boards can be accessed. Report on how to access one of these bulletin boards, the types of information it contains, costs, and who maintains it. Use WORKSHEET 11.2 to organize this information.

4. Contact local users' groups or the community library for listings of public-domain programs available. Another source is the school district office. Report on five programs that are available, how they can be obtained, and who is responsible for maintaining the list of software.

5. Investigate an information utility. You may want to research one related to your career choice. Your local library or computer store may have a list available. Use WORKSHEET 11.3 to help you organize the information. This project relates to "Applying What You've Learned" problem #3.

6. WHAT DO YOU THINK? How could an electronic bulletin board be misused? What kinds of information should not be put on a bulletin board? How could people using the board protect against misuse?

WORKSHEETS

11.1 Modem specifications

11.2 Bulletin board information

11.3 Information utility

REFERENCES

All About Modems. Delran, NJ: Data Pro Research, 1971- (directory).

All About Multiplexers. Delran, NJ: Data Pro Research, 1974- (directory).

Barr, Robert E. "Are EDI and EFT in your tax filing future?", *Journal of Systems Management*, April, 1991, pp. 32-34.

Dewey, Patrick R. *Essential Guide to Bulletin Board Systems.* Westport, CT: Meckler: 1987.

Madron, Thomas W. *Local Area Networks: The Next Generation (2nd ed.)* New York: John Wiley and Sons, 1990.

Martin, James. *Telecommunications and the Computer (3rd ed).* Englewood Cliffs, NJ: Prentice-Hall, 1990.

O'Dell, Peter. *The Computer Networking Book.* Chapel Hill, NC: Ventana Press: 1989.

Rogers, Michael. "Smart cards: Pocket power", *Newsweek*, July 31, 1989, pp. 54-55.

Sherman, Kenneth. *Data Communication User Guide.*, Englewood Cliffs, NJ: Prentice-Hall, 1990.

Stover, Dawn. "World without wires", *Popular Science*, April, 1990, pp. 100-114.

Data Communications

MIX AND MATCH

Match the following terms with the definitions below.
Each question has only one answer.

a. acoustic coupler
b. analog signal
c. asynchronous
d. baud rate
e. BBS
f. BPS
g. bus topology
h. communication channel
i. concentrator
j. data communication
k. digital signal
l. direct-connect modem
m. download
n. EFT
o. facsimile machine
p. file server
q. gateway
r. hard-wired
s. host
t. hybrid topology
u. information utility
v. LAN
w. modem
x. multiplexer
y. network topologies
z. node
aa. ring topology
bb. smart card
cc. smart modems
dd. star topology
ee. synchronous
ff. telecommunications
gg. telecommuting
hh. teleconferencing
ii. upload
jj. VAN
kk. WAN

_____ 1. electronic signals expressing bit patterns

_____ 2. type of modem designed to hold a regular phone

_____ 3. electronic signals expressing patterns of continuous sound frequencies

_____ 4. modems containing processing capabilities

_____ 5. hardware acting as a switching station for communication signals

_____ 6. data transmission pattern where data is sent byte by byte

_____ 7. hardware that converts signals; between analog and digital formats

_____ 8. measurement of the number of signal changes an analog signal can make in a specific period of time

_____ 9. central computer in a star network

CHAPTER 11

_____ 10. disk drive servicing computers in a network containing data and programs common to many users

_____ 11. medium for data communication

_____ 12. data transmission pattern where data is grouped into a block before sending

_____ 13. hardware that saves transmissions, sending them as a group

_____ 14. private network spread over a large area

_____ 15. computer system within a network

_____ 16. topology connecting several nodes with a single communication channel

_____ 17. transfer data or programs to another computer

_____ 18. private network within a small area

_____ 19. components physically connected by wires

_____ 20. topology containing a central computer connected to all nodes

_____ 21. public access message systems on computers

_____ 22. general models for communication networks

_____ 23. topology connecting nodes in a large circle

_____ 24. combination of several topologies

_____ 25. type of modem directly connected to phone jack

_____ 26. transfer data or programs from the host computer to a node

_____ 27. commercial service providing online information

_____ 28. sending documents or messages through communication lines

_____ 29. interface connecting various networks to each other

_____ 30. exchange of financial transaction data

_____ 31. credit card containing a processor and memory

Data Communications

_____ 32. network providing information service for a fee

_____ 33. measurement of transfer speed over communication lines

_____ 34. sending data over long distances

_____ 35. device that transmits photos and drawings over communication lines

_____ 36. transmission of job assignments and completed work over communication lines

_____ 37. exchange of ideas by a large group of people over communication lines

Chapter 11

by A. Walters

ACROSS

2. Transferring data or programs to another computer.
4. The central computer in a star network.
8. A measurement of data transmission speed where the number of zero or one digits per second is measured. (3 words, with 3 down)
9. A wide area network with additional services available to users, like access to databases and electronic mail. (abbr.)
10. A modem that attaches to a telephone handset. (2 words)
11. A public or private network covering a large geographic area. (abbr.)
12. A sophisticated multiplexer which stores the signals to be transmitted in groups.
13. ____ topology. A network where each node is connected to two other nodes forming a circle.
16. ____ topology. A network where all nodes are interconnected to each other through a single communications channel.
18. A device that combines signals from several incoming transmissions to be sent to a computer.
19. A collection of terminals, computers, and transmission devices connected for data communication.
20. Receiving data of programs from another computer.
21. ____ transmission. Data transmission that involves only oneway communication, like a public address system.
23. Communications channel that performs wireless data transfer at 20–35 mile distances and handles data at 1–3 million bps.
24. An interface between a LAN and another network.
25. ____ modem. A stand alone modem.

DOWN

1. ____ ____ interchange. Organizations exchanging data such as customer lists, orders, and banking information. (2 words)
2. ____ ____ modem. A modem installed inside the computer or is physically attached to the computer. (2 words)
3. (2nd half of 3 down)
5. (2nd half of 14 down)
6. Communication channel that is used for cable television and transmites data at 1-million bps. (2 words)
7. Data transmission mode where data is sent a by byte at a time surrounded by start and stop bits.
8. Rate at which data is transmitted through a modem. It is measured as the speed in which a signal changes over a period of time. (2 words)
13. Signal which record data as a series of bit patterns. (2 words, with 5 down)
15. Physically connected by wire or cable.
17. A device which converts data between analog and digital signals.
19. One computer system within a communications network.
21. ____ topology. A network with one central computer, which has all nodes attached only to it.
22. ____ communication sending data electronically from one location to another.

Data Communications

WORKSHEET: 11.1
PROJECT: 2   Name:_____

_____
SPECIAL COMMUNICATIONS SOFTWARE (if any):

_____
ASYNCHRONOUS OR SYNCHROUNOUS:

_____
AVAILABLE BAUD RATE:

_____
FULL OR HALF DUPLEX:

_____
PARITY (Even, Odd, or None):

_____
DATATBITS (7 or 8 bits/byte):

_____
STOPBITS (1 or 2):

_____
COMPUTER'S TELEPHONE NUMBER:

_____
CONTACT AT COMPUTER CENTER:
              TELEPHONE #:

CHAPTER 11

WORKSHEET: 11.2
PROJECT: 3

Name:_____

BULLETIN BOARD

Bulletin Board Name:

Access Phone No.: | Baud Rate:

Hours Available:

Sysop (System Operator) or Contact Person:

Board location, if known:

Address for futher information:

Board specializes in: | LOGON Procedure:

Any rules, regulations for access:

Data Communications

WORKSHEET: 11.3
PROJECT: 5

Name: _____

INFORMATION UTILITY

Utility Name:

Contact Name/Address for Information:

Access Phone No.:	Baud Rate:
Hours Available:	Rate Structure
Types of Information Available:	LOGON Procedure:
Access Rules/Regulations:	

CLASS NOTES

CHAPTER 12: MANAGEMENT AND DECISION SUPPORT SYSTEMS

PURPOSE

Computer-based management informations systems are examined as to make-up, operation, and applications in an organization. The use of decision support systems and expert systems are discussed. All material is presented in relation to the level of management it best serves.

TERMS TO REMEMBER

authoring system
backward chaining
decision support system (DSS)
detailed report
exception report
executive
executive information system
expert system
forward chaining
front-line management
inference engine
knowledge base

knowledge engineer
linear programming
management information system (MIS)
middle management
model
operational decision
strategic decision
summary report
tactical decision
top management
transaction cycle
user interface

ANSWERS TO REVIEW QUESTIONS

1. Define each "term to remember".

   authoring system -

   backward chaining -

   decision support system (DSS) -

   detailed report -

   exception report -

executive -

executive information system -

expert system -

forward chaining -

front-line management -

inference engine -

knowledge base -

knowledge engineer -

linear programming -

management information system (MIS) -

middle management -

model -

operational decision -

strategic decision -

summary report -

tactical decision -

top management -

transaction cycle -

user interface -

2. What is the role of management in an organization?

3. What types of decisions and problems do the three levels of management handle?

4. Describes the differences between financial, personnel, research, and production/sales data.

   Financial data -

   Personnel data -

   Research data -

   Production/sales data -

5. What types of reports do the different levels of management need to perform their jobs?

6. How are models and queries used as part of decision support systems?

7. What is an advantage and a disadvantage to using linear programming models?

8. What types of questions do query languages help users to answer?

9. How can electronic mail support decision making?

10. Identify four ways spreadsheets can help decision makers.

    1.

    2.

    3.

    4.

11. How do graphics packages support the decision making process?

12. Identify the three components of an expert system and explain how each works.

    1.

    2.

    3.

13. Describe applications for forward and backward chaining.

    forward chaining -

    backward chaining -

14. How can expert systems assist experienced and inexperienced people?

15. Why are expert systems difficult to develop?

16. What types of problems are expert systems designed to handle?

17. When is it practical to develop an expert system?

PROJECTS

1. For an organization familiar to you (related to school, a job, hobby, or career), use WORKSHEET 12.1 to examine the levels of management and the types of decisions made. For each type of management, describe the duties involved. Also list examples of decisions at each level.

2. Find an article on an expert system now in existence or one being developed. Write a summary of the article listing the types of information involved, which experts are being consulted, how long the development takes, and any problems involved in setting up the expert system.

3. Several tools are available for decision makers, from electronic spreadsheets to expert systems. Compare the tools mentioned in the text by listing some advantages/ disadvantages and what types of organizations could benefit most from these tools. Use WORKSHEET 12.2 to help you.

4. WHAT DO YOU THINK? A DSS computer simulation with incorrect data wrongly predicted the movement of a cloud of toxic gas over a chemical plant in West Virginia. Over 130 people were hospitalized as a result. Who should be held responsible: the chemical company? the people involved in collecting the data? the data entry operator? the data entry supervisor? the programmer of the simulation? no one?

WORKSHEETS

12.1 Listing of decision makers and decision types for an organization

12.2 Comparison of manual MIS, computerized MIS, DSS, expert system, and electronic spreadsheet

REFERENCES

Campbell, Kathy. "Choosing an executive information system", *Information Management*, May, 1991, pp. 30+.

Kelly-Bootle, Stan. "The devil's AI dictionary", *AI Expert*, April 1991, pp. 153-162.

Kidd, Alison L. (Ed.). *Knowledge Acquisition for Expert Systems: A Practical Handbook*. New York: Plenum Press, 1987.

Partridge, D. *Artificial Intelligence: Applications in the Future of Software Engineering*. New York: Halsted Press, 1986.

Rushinek, Avi and Rushinek, Sara. "DSS software evaluation and selection.", *Information Executive*, Spring 1991, pp. 40-45.

Ruth, Christopher and Steve Ruth. *Developing Expert Systems Using 1st-CLASS*. Santa Cruz, CA: Mitchell Publishing, 1988.

Sprague, Kristopher and Steve Ruth. *Developing Expert Systems Using EXSYS*. Santa Cruz, CA: Mitchell Publishing, 1988.

Umbaugh, Robert E. (Ed.) *The Handbook of MIS Management.* Boston, MA: Auerbach, 1985- (handbook).

Walson, Hugh J. and Rainer, R. Kelly Jr. "A manager's guide to executive support systems", *Business Horizons*, March/April, 1991, pp. 44-50.

Watkins, Ronald W. "Decision support delivers bottom line results", *Information Executive*, Spring 1991, pp. 20-21.

Management and Decision Support Systems

MIX AND MATCH

Match the following terms with the definitions below.
Each question has only one answer.

a. authoring system
b. backward chaining
c. DSS
d. detailed report
e. exception report
f. executive
g. executive information system
h. expert system
i. forward chaining
j. front-line management
k. inference engine
l. knowledge base

m. knowledge engineer
n. linear programming
o. MIS
p. middle management
q. model
r. operational decision
s. strategic decision
t. summary report
u. tactical decision
v. top management
w. transaction cycle
x. user interface

_____ 1. the input, processing, output, and storage of a single transaction

_____ 2. person who works with human experts to create a knowledge base

_____ 3. DSS that aids top-level management in strategic decisions

_____ 4. network of systems providing information to an organization's decision makers

_____ 5. management level with day-to-day control and responsibilities

_____ 6. report showing specific information about an activity or event

_____ 7. software to help customize user interface and associated data management system

_____ 8. people who manage intermediate levels of detail

_____ 9. decisions on short-term (but not day-to-day) organizational goals

_____ 10. real-time computer system aiding managers in solving problems

CHAPTER 12

_____ 11. problem solving approach used by expert system which starts with a problem and tries to find possible causes

_____ 12. report totaling information about an activity or event

_____ 13. decisions on day-to-day transactions

_____ 14. method of finding an optimum solution for a problem by presenting constraints

_____ 15. people who manage global goals for organization

_____ 16. decisions on long-term organizational goals

_____ 17. report listing situations meeting specific conditions

_____ 18. mathematical representation of a problem

_____ 19. rules for how experts make decisions

_____ 20. the user friendly features of a DSS: natural language query system, menus, and help screens

_____ 21. software for an expert system

_____ 22. computer system that simulates human thought and judgment

_____ 23. problem solving approach used by expert system which starts with known causes and identifies the problem

_____ 24. another name for the executive management level

Chapter 12

by A. Walters

ACROSS

2. (chpt. 6) Software feature that allows the user to see at the same time parts of the worksheet that are not adjacent.
5. (second word with 25 across)
7. Another word for textual data. (chpt. 1)
9. (2nd word with 11 across)
10. (2nd word with 19 down)
11. A report that condenses or totals detailed items to show trends. (with 9 across)
12. (2nd part with 10 down)
14. ____ management. People who make long-term strategic decisions involving wide ranging effects.
15. Software that retrieves data and makes decisions based on a set of rules using data and probabilities from an integrated knowledge base. (2 words)
17. (with 26 across)
20. (with 21 down, 2 words)
23. ____ decision. Long term decision made by executives that determines how an organization is going to achieve its' goals.
24. A mathematical representation of an organizational situation.
25. A real-time computer system that helps managers solve problems through data retrieval and modeling. (1st word with 5 across)
26. A type of modeling where an optimum solution for a problem is found for a given system of requirements and constraints. (1st word with 17 across)
27. A report showing one output line for each item in a file or database. (2 words)

DOWN

1. (chpt. 6) Command to leave the spreadsheet software and enter another package or the operating system.
3. (chpt. 5) The rolling of text up, down, and sideways on a screen for viewing long or wide documents.
4. ____ decision. Short term decision made by middle managers that impacts when, where and how an organization's resources are used.
6. Facts and figures about employees and their productivity. (2 words)
7. The input, processing, output, and storage of a single transaction. (2 words)
8. People who make operational decisions about daily activities in the organization. (3 words)
10. Goal-driven problem-solving approach used by expert systems which starts with a problem (goal) and works backwards to identify possible causes. (1st word with 12 across)
13. (chpt. 5) Style of printed character.
16. ____ system. A user interface, inference engine, and knowledge base which contain decision making rules and probabilities for expected outcomes.
18. Another name for a person at top mgt level.
19. Collections of information containing data about a specific domain along with probabilities. (1st word with 10 across)
21. A combination of user-friendly features to make a decision support system or expert system available to users. (1st word with 20 across)
22. ____ data. Facts and figures about past performance and plans for future projects.

CHAPTER 12

WORKSHEET: 12.1
PROJECT: 1

Name:_____

ORGANIZATION:

MANAGEMENT LEVEL	DUTIES	DECISIONS
FRONT-LINE		
MIDDLE		
TOP (EXECUTIVE)		

Management and Decision Support Systems

WORKSHEET: 12.2
PROJECT: 3

Name:_____

INFORMATION TOOL	POTENTIAL USERS	ADVANTAGE	DISADVANTAGE
MANUAL MANAGEMENT INFORMATION SYSTEM			
COMPUTERIZED MANAGEMENT INFORMATION SYSTEM			
DECISION SUPPORT SYSTEM			
EXPERT SYSTEM			
ELECTRONIC SPREADSHEET			

CLASS NOTES

CHAPTER 13: SYSTEMS DESIGN AND IMPLEMENTATION

PURPOSE

In this chapter, systems development is divided into four life cycle steps. Each step is discussed in detail by looking at the phases involved. Applications of these steps to both multiuser and personal computer systems are covered.

TERMS TO REMEMBER

application development team
CASE (computer-aided software engineering) tools
contract programmer
conversion
cost/benefit analysis
critical path
data flow diagram
direct cutover
feasibility study
gantt chart
initial review
installation
life cycle
maintenance
parallel operation
PERT (program evaluation and review technique)
phased transition
pilot operation
print chart
project management software
prototyping
record layout form
request for proposal (RFP)
screen layout form
service bureau
system specifications
systems development project
systems test

ANSWERS TO REVIEW QUESTIONS

1. Define each "term to remember."

    application development team -

    CASE (computer-aided software engineering) tools -

    contract programmers -

    conversion -

cost/benefit analysis -

critical path -

data flow diagram -

direct cutover -

feasibility study -

gantt chart -

initial review -

installation -

life cycle -

maintenance -

parallel operation -

PERT (Program Evaluation and Review Technique) -

phased transition -

pilot operation -

print chart -

project management software -

prototyping -

record layout form -

request for proposal (RFP) -

screen layout form -

service bureau -

system specifications -

systems development project -

system test -

2. What were two of the major obstacles that created problems with the development of early computer systems?

   1.

   2.

3. Explain how systems development projects are made more manageable.

4. What special precautions should be added to the systems development process to help ensure success?

5. Identify the four steps in the life cycle of a systems development project.

   1.

   2.

   3.

   4.

6. What usually initiates the development of a new computer system?

7. Who performs an initial review, and what are their responsibilities?

Systems Design and Implementation

8. Who determines if a new computer system has merit and initiates the feasibility study?

9. Who would be a member of an application development team during the feasibility study phase?

10. What information-gathering techniques are part of the feasibility study?

11. Explain the 80-20 rule.

12. What are the results of a feasibility study?

13. Describe how the requirements step applies to the purchase of a personal computer system.

14. Why does the application development team provide management with a list of alternative system solutions?

191

15. What are three intangible costs and benefits managers must consider when evaluating system alternatives?

    1.

    2.

    3.

16. What decisions are made in the final phase of the alternative evaluation step?

17. What decisions are made when evaluating alternatives for a personal computer system?

18. Name two advantages and three disadvantages of prototyping.

    Advantages

    1.

    2.

    Disadvantages

    1.

    2.

    3.

19. Identify an advantage and two disadvantages of using CASE tools.

    Advantage

    Disadvantages

    1.

    2.

20. What is the purpose of a data encyclopedia in a CASE toolkit?

21. Use the components of a computer system to describe the activities and requirements that make up a set of system specifications.

    Hardware:

    Programs:

    Data:

    Procedures:

    People:

22. What happens at the end of the design step?

23. What activities are involved in designing a personal computer system?

24. Who would be a member of an application development team during the construction phase of implementation?

25. What happens during the construction phase?

26. Who needs to be trained before the system test can occur?

27. Why are people trained during the installation phase?

28. What is the purpose of the immediate and six month follow-up reviews of a completed system development project?

Systems Design and Implementation

29. Why are some system modifications left to the maintenance phase?

30. Describe the steps in the life cycle of a systems development process. Be sure to identify the phases associated with each step.

   1.

      phases:

   2.

      phases:

   3.

      phases:

   4.

      phases:

31. What steps are included in the set up and maintenance of a new personal computer system?

195

32. Explain the features common to project management software.

PROJECTS

1. Find one or more ads for a systems analyst position. What kinds of educational requirements, work experience, and salary are stated? What kinds of personality traits would make a person an effective systems analyst?

2. In the design step, each of the five computer system components must be considered. For the applications found on WORKSHEET 13.1, write out a list of possible specifications or requirements needed for each component. Assume that no computer system exists at present.

3. Use WORKSHEET 13.2 to work through a systems development process for purchasing a microcomputer system for your personal use. Follow the life cycle steps and their associated phases as given in the text.

4. WHAT DO YOU THINK? Systems development can be a long complicated process, sometimes taking several years to complete. Look at each of the four life cycle steps.

    a) If that step were left out of the process, what are some possible implications?

    b) Could the plan succeed without that step?

WORKSHEETS

13.1 Specifications for five components

13.2 Systems development for a personal computer system

REFERENCES

Callan, John P. "Who needs maintenance tools?", *Technical Support*, June, 1991, pp. 27-29.

Hanna, Mary Alice. "Prototyping helps users get design satisfaction", *software Magazine*, April, 1991, pp. 43-44+.

Hetzen, William C. *The Complete Guide to Software Testing*. Wellesley, MA: QED Information Services, 1984.

Kolodner, Janet L. "Improving human decision making through CASE-based decision aiding", *AI Magazine*, Summer, 1991, pp. 52-68.

Liebowitz, Jay. "When is a prototype an expert system?", *Expert System*, Spring, 1991, pp. 17-22.

Pitman, Ben. "Technical and people sides of systems project start-up", *Journal of Systems Management*, April, 1991, pp. 6-8.

Taylor, Lee. "39 questions to successful systems designs.". *Information Center*, February 1985, pp. 36-43+.

Tech, Robert S., Sr. and Kathy Brittain White. "Team effectiveness in systems analysis." *Interface: The Computer Education Quarterly*, Spring 1985, pp. 8-10.

Ware, Robb. "Project management software: The silver bullet?", *Journal of Systems Management*, May, 1991, p. 20.

CHAPTER 13

MIX AND MATCH

Match the following terms with the definitions below.
Each question has only one answer.

a. application development team
b. CASE tools
c. contract programmer
d. conversion
e. cost/benefit analysis
f. critical path
g. data flow diagram
h. direct cutover
i. feasibility study
j. gantt chart
k. initial review
l. installation
m. life cycle
n. maintenance
o. parallel operation
p. PERT
q. phased transition
r. pilot operation
s. print chart
t. project management software
u. prototyping
v. record layout form
w. RFP
x. screen layout form
y. service bureau
z. system specifications
aa. system development project
bb. system test

_____ 1. steps taken to define and create new systems

_____ 2. study to determine whether a project is realistic

_____ 3. installation method where all of the new system is installed in part of the organization

_____ 4. diagram of how printed output will look

_____ 5. outside agency providing data processing services

_____ 6. project structure that break down a system development into four steps

_____ 7. installation method where both old and new systems are running simultaneously

_____ 8. description of methods and results for new systems

_____ 9. diagram of how screen output will look

_____ 10. report identifying source of a system problem and if there is a computer-based solution

_____ 11. group of users and analysts that gather information about a potential project

Systems Design and Implementation

_____ 12. diagram of record organization and fields

_____ 13. starting up (operating) a new computer system

_____ 14. installation method where part of the new system is installed in the entire organization

_____ 15. visual representation of relationship between people and data

_____ 16. report comparing cost and benefits for each system alterative

_____ 17. list of specifications with request to vendors for bid on system

_____ 18. temporary programmers hired to do a specific job

_____ 19. installation method where old system stops and new system starts with no overlap

_____ 20. any modification to an operating computer system

_____ 21. diagram showing a timeline for steps in the system development life cycle

_____ 22. another name for installation

_____ 23. these charts show the order and time requirements for each task in a project as boxes connected by lines

_____ 24. software to develop systems projects through using a data encyclopedia to generate timelines, reports, and diagrams.

_____ 25. combination of events in a PERT chart that require the maximum time

_____ 26. a test of the operation of the new system using real data

_____ 27. modeling user interfaces like screens and reports

_____ 28. integrated software containing scheduling, cost estimation, resource management and other features

Chapter 13

by A. Walters

ACROSS

1. (chpt. 5) User blocks off text which can then be moved or copied to another part of a file. (3 words)
6. (chpt. 5) Automatic replacement of all occurrences of a word or phrase in a word processed document without user involvement. (2 words)
7. Service ____. An outside agency that provides computer services.
9. Charts that show the order and time requirements for each task in a project as boxes connected by lines. (abbr.)
12. Programmers temporarily employed by organizations to work on a systems development project. (2 words)
14. A study done by a systems analyst to identify a problem and see if it has a computer-based solution.
16. Software that helps systems analysts develope computer systems by integrating through a data encyclopedia various diagramming and charting tools. (abbr.) (2 words, with 26 across)
19. ____ transition. A piecemeal approach to conversion of part of the system. It is put into operation throughout the entire organization, other parts are added in stages.
21. ____ operation. A type of installation where the entire new system is tried in just a small part of the organization.
22. Method of conversion where the old system is removed and the new system is immediately brought in. (2 words, with 20 down)
23. ____ benefit analysis. A report presenting both tangible and intangible costs and benefits of a systems project.
24. Description of a system specifications accompanying request for bids by vendors. (3 words, with 11 down)
25. System ____. A test of the operation of the new system under real conditions using real data.
26. (2nd word with 16 across).

DOWN

1. (chpt. 6) A spreadsheet function which a user retrieves with a few keystrokes.
2. (chpt. 6) Intersection of a worksheet row and column containing numbers, formulas, or text.
3. (chpt. 6) Command that duplicates contents of a cell, row or column to another location.
4. (chpt. 5) Short line segment added to type style which helps eye flow across line of printed text.
5. ____ chart. A chart showing starting dates and duration for different activities in the system development process.
8. A form that shows how data fields will be organized into records in a file. (3 words)
9. ____ ____ software. An integrated software package containing scheduling, cost estimation, resource management, and other tools to aid in coordinating projects. (2 words)
10. Application development ____. A group responsible for conducting the feasibility study and doing further work on a systems development project.
11. (3rd word of 24 across)
12. Changing from an old system to a new computer system.
13. Keeping to one or more of a computer system's components up-to-date.
15. ____ ____ form. A form that shows how output will appear on a screen. (2 words)
17. ____ cycle. A structure for a project that divides a large job into a series of smaller steps.
18. ____ chart. A form that shows how output will appear on paper.
20. (2nd word with 22 across)

Systems Design and Implementation

WORKSHEET: 13.1
PROJECT: 2

Name: _____

SYSTEM COMPONENTS	SCHOOL RECORDS (classes, grades, etc.)	FAST FOOD RESTAURANT (orders, inventory, etc.)
DATA		
PROGRAMS		
HARDWARE		
PEOPLE		
PROCEDURES		

201

CHAPTER 13

WORKSHEET: 13.2
PROJECT: 3, page 1

Name: _____

STEP 1: REQUIREMENTS

A. How computer will be used:	B. Software needs:
C. Location of new system:	D. Users:

STEP 2: ALTERNATIVES

A. System components:
  Minimum memory:
  Operating system:
  Diskette drives:
  Hard drives:
  Keyboard type:
  Expansion slots:
  Color/BW monitor:
  Printer:

B. Costs (in addition to components)

   -supplies   -estimated learning time

C. Benefits

Systems Design and Implementation

WORKSHEET: 13.2
PROJECT: 3, page 2

Name:_____

STEP 3: DESIGN

A. Update system components list to include source, model name, price

B. Documentation included with system:

C. Training included with system:

D. Warranties included with system:

E. Timeline for purchases:

STEP 4. IMPLEMENTATION AND MAINTENANCE

A. Setup details

   Workspace:

   Disk storage:

   Manual storage:

   Lighting:

   Surge protector:

   Other:

B. Maintenance schedule

   Clean disk heads:

   Clean printer:

   Cover keyboard:

   Backup files:

   Other:

CLASS NOTES

CHAPTER 14: SOFTWARE DEVELOPMENT

PURPOSE

Program development from its design, through coding and testing, is presented in this chapter. Common programming languages and tools for program design are also discussed.

TERMS TO REMEMBER

bug
code
debugging
flowchart
hierarchy chart
module
object-oriented programming (OOP)
program specifications
pseudocode
repetition
selection
sequence
structure chart
structured program
structured walkthrough
stub testing
test data
unstructured program
version

ANSWERS TO REVIEW QUESTIONS

1. Define each "term to remember".

    bug -

    code -

    debugging -

    flowchart -

    hierarchy chart -

    module -

object-oriented programming (OOP) -

program specifications -

pseudocode -

repetition -

selection -

sequence -

structure chart -

structured program -

structured walkthrough -

stub testing -

test data -

unstructured program -

version -

2. What are the four skills programmers use to develop software?

    1.

    2.

    3.

    4.

3. In what ways is computer programming different from the misconceptions people have about the programming process?

4. Identify the four steps in the programming process.

    1.

    2.

    3.

    4.

5. Why is an unstructured program sometimes referred to as spaghetti code?

6. Describe two ways the program development process changed during the 1970s.

7. Identify the three structures found in a structured program.

    1.

    2.

    3.

8. How is a program module different from an object?

9. What is meant by the statement "programs are designed from the top down"?

10. What are two advantages of using structure charts, flowcharts, or pseudocode to design a program?

    1.

    2.

11. How do structured walkthroughs help reduce costs and enhance program quality?

12. How does a line of pseudocode or a flowcharting symbol relate to program code?

Software Development

13. Describe two activities that help programmers check the reliability of their programs.

14. Identify the strengths, weaknesses (if available), and types of applications associated with these programming languages: FORTRAN, COBOL, BASIC, LOGO, Pascal, Ada, C, RPG, fourth generation languages, and natural languages.

   FORTRAN -

   Strengths:

   Weaknesses:

   COBOL -

   Strengths:

   Weaknesses:

   BASIC -

   Strengths:

   Weaknesses:

   LOGO -

   Strengths:

   Weaknesses:

   Pascal -

   Strengths:

   Weaknesses:

Ada -

  Strengths:

  Weaknesses:

C -

  Strengths:

  Weaknesses:

RPG -

  Strengths:

  Weaknesses:

fourth generation languages -

  Strengths:

  Weaknesses:

natural languages -

  Strengths:

  Weaknesses:

15. What activities are associated with a system test?

16. How can the design of structured programs help in program maintenance?

17. What is one requirement for a realistic system test?

18. Identify two reasons why program documentation is important.

    1.

    2.

19. What happens during a documentation review?

20. What is program maintenance?

PROJECTS

1. What programming languages are available on your school's computer? Are they translated by compilers or interpreters (see chapter 4)? What documentation (manuals, tutorials, etc.) is included with the language? What applications or classes could benefit from using these languages?

2. Collect three job advertisements for programmers. What are the educational and experience requirements? What languages are involved? What types of applications are being programmed? What are the salaries?

3. Articles have been written about structured programming and object-oriented programming. Review an article on one of these techniques and list associated advantages and disadvantages.

4. Create a flowchart and pseudocode for each of the three
   programming structures (sequence, selection, and repetition)
   as they relate to one of the following events:

   a. looking for a job
   b. putting names in alphabetical order
   c. printing the list of students on academic probation
   d. baking a cake

   Use WORKSHEET 14.1 and information in the text or a
   programming text to help you.

5. WHAT DO YOU THINK? Someone once said, "I don't want
   software that is user friendly; I want software that is easy
   to use". Rank the following features in how useful they
   would be to you as a beginning user.

   a. pull-down menus
   b. windows
   c. context sensitive help screens
   d. prompts displaying program options
   e. on-line tutorials

   Now rerank them as you think an experienced user would.

WORKSHEETS

14.1 Flowcharts and pseudocode for the three programming
     structures

REFERENCES

Becker, Pete. "Testing, testing...", *Computer Language*, April,
   1991, pp. 59-64.

Berztiss, Alfs. *Programming with Generators: An Introduction.*
   Englewood Cliffs, NJ: Prentice-Hall, 1990.

Crenshaw, Jack W. "A perfect marriage", *Computer Languages*,
   June, 1991, pp. 44-48+.

Goff, Leslie. "Programming in the future", *InformationWeek*, June
   24, 1991, pp. 36-37+.

Grimm, Susan J. *How to Write Computer Documentation for Users
   (2nd ed.).* New York: Van Nostrand Reinhold, 1986.

Hobby, Jim. "Testing software quality", *PC Business Software*, vol. 16, no. 1, pp. 8-13.

Horowitz, Ellis (Ed.). *Programming Languages: A Grand Tour* (2nd ed.). Rockville, MD: Computer Science Press, 1985.

Johnson, Bruce and Ruwe, Marcia. *Professional Programming in COBOL.* Englewood Cliffs, NJ: 1991.

Ledin, George Jr. and Victor Ledin. *The Programmer's Book of Rules.* Belmont, CA: Lifetime Learning, 1984.

Papert, Seymour. *Mindstorms.* New York: Basic Books, 1980.

Perry, William E. *A Standard for Testing Application Software.* Boston, MA: Auerbach Publishers, 1985- (reference service).

Rodgers, Ulka. "DBMS-independent 4GLs", *Database Programming and Design*, May 1991, pp. 58-62+.

Shamlin, Carolyn. *The Other Side of Software: A User's Guide for Defining Software Requirements (2nd ed.).* New York: AMACOM, 1990.

Smith, Truch. *Secrets of Software Debugging.* Blue Ridge Summit, PA: TAB Books, 1984.

Software Encyclopedia, The. 2 volumes, Bowker, 1990.

"Term paper: An object-oriented glossary", *Computerworld*, April 22, 1991. p. 84.

MIX AND MATCH

Match the following terms with the definitions below.
Each question has only one answer.

a. bug
b. code
c. debugging
d. flowchart
e. hierarchy chart
f. module
g. OOP
h. program specifications
i. pseudocode
j. repetition
k. selection
l. sequence
m. structure chart
n. structured program
o. structured walkthrough
p. stub testing
q. test data
r. unstructured program
s. version

_____ 1. written program instructions

_____ 2. specific details for designing a program

_____ 3. programs written with a linear approach

_____ 4. programs written in modules using only three structures

_____ 5. program structure where instructions are executed in order written

_____ 6. program structure where one of two alternatives is chosen

_____ 7. program structure where a group of instructions is repeated as needed

_____ 8. a set of instructions performing a single function

_____ 9. graphic representation of a module (its relationship) within a program

_____ 10. box and arrow diagram showing program flow

_____ 11. English phrases used in an outline to describe program flow

_____ 12. step-by-step review of program design by a team

_____ 13. sets of data that include extremes as well as normal operating data

Software Development

_____ 14. programming methodology where data and program logic are organized into objects

_____ 15. errors within coded program

_____ 16. finding and correcting errors in programs

_____ 17. testing one module at a time

_____ 18. different edition of a program

_____ 19. another name for hierarchy chart

Chapter 14

by A. Walters

28. ____ programming. Programming methodology where is organized into objects, each containing both the data and processing operations.

DOWN

1. Each new edition of software and documentation. (pl.)
2. Section of program code in object-oriented programming that contains both the processing code and related data to perform more complex functions.
3. Structured ____. A program organized to contain only three logical structures.
4. A subset of a program containing processing code that only performs a single function.
6. The ongoing procedure of making modifications to software based on changes in laws or company policy. (2 words)
7. High level programming language used in education and on micros and minis.
9. The process of finding and correct program errors.
12. A graphic representation of the relationship among the modules or objects in a structured program. (1st word with 19 across)
13. A method of representing program logic by using different symbols and arrows.
14. Programming language used for decision support and expert systems. (1st word with 22 across)
18. (chpt. 6) Software feature that allows the user to see at the same time parts of the worksheet that are not adjacent.
23. High level programming language used in scientific applications, especially by the Department of Defense.
26. Written program instructions.

ACROSS

5. Sequence of instructions is repeated until some processing condition is changed.
6. Part of the software development cycle that tests program modules, complete programs, and the entire system under realistic operating conditions. (2 words, with 20 across)
7. An error within a coded program.
8. High level programming language used in business report generating applications.
10. Instructions are executed in the order they appear in the program.
11. Programming language used for business applications.
13. High level programming language used for scientific and mathematical applications.
15. High level programming language used in education.
17. Part of a program development cycle where all documentation is gone over in detail by the project manager, director of computer operations, and the data librarian. (2 words)
19. (2nd word with 12 down)
20. (2nd word with 6 across)
21. High level programming language used in education and for scientific purposes.
22. (2nd word with 14 down)
24. (chpt. 6) Command that duplicates contents of a cell, row, or column to another location.
25. Sets of data used for program testing that represent all extremes and normal conditions the program would experience. (2 words)
27. A method of representing program logic by using English phrases in an outline.

Software Development

WORKSHEET: 14.1
PROJECT: 4

Name:_____

APPLICATION:

FLOWCHART	PSEUDOCODE
SEQUENCE	
SELECTION	
REPETITION	

CLASS NOTES

CHAPTER 15: PRIVACY, ETHICS, CRIME, AND SECURITY

PURPOSE

The laws supporting privacy of personal data are reviewed the fundamentals of ethical behavior related to technology are discussed. Also, warning signals for potential computer crime for both large and small computer systems, types of crimes, and prevention through security measures are discussed in this chapter.

TERMS TO REMEMBER

activity log
antivirus software
control totals
copy protection
data encryption
electronic data processing (EDP) controls

ethical standard
password
virus
write protect
write protect notch
write-protect window

ANSWERS TO REVIEW QUESTIONS

1. Define each "term to remember".

    activity log -

    antivirus software -

    control totals -

    copy protection -

    data encryption -

    electronic data processing (EDP) controls -

ethical standard -

password -

virus -

write protect -

write protect notch -

write-protect window -

2. When can a creditor legally invade a person's privacy?

3. Describe the rights defined by the following:

Fourth Amendment -

Freedom of Information Act of 1970 -

Fair Credit Reporting Act of 1970 -

Privacy Act of 1974 -

Privacy, Ethics, Crime, and Security

Education Privacy Act of 1974 -

Right to Financial Privacy Act of 1978 -

Electronic Communications Privacy Act of 1986 -

Video Privacy Protection Act of 1988 -

4. Why would an organization establish ethical guidelines?

5. Identify 12 questions you should consider before taking potentially unethical actions?

   1.
   2.
   3.
   4.
   5.
   6.
   7.
   8.
   9.
   10.
   11.
   12.

6. What are two means of controlling computer impact?

   1.

   2.

7. Identify five types of computer crime.

   1.

   2.

   3.

   4.

   5.

8. Why would an organization be reluctant to prosecute computer criminals?

9. What are 11 warning signals of computer crime?

   1.

   2.

   3.

   4.

   5.

   6.

   7.

   8.

   9.

   10.

   11.

Privacy, Ethics, Crime, and Security

10. How are computer-oriented worms, trojans, and bombs different from a virus?

    virus -

    worm -

    trojan -

    bomb -

11. Identify two procedures you can use to protect a computer system from destructive programs?

    1.

    2.

12. What are six warning signs of an infected computer system?

    1.
    2.
    3.
    4.
    5.
    6.

13. What type of physical security is provided by copy protection and data encryption?

223

14. What are nine types of physical controls that can be used to secure a computer system?

   1.

   2.

   3.

   4.

   5.

   6.

   7.

   8.

   9.

15. How is a write-protect notch and write-protect window used to safeguard data on disks?

16. How can data be protected after access to a computer system has been established?

17. How are computer crimes often discovered?

Privacy, Ethics, Crime, and Security

18. Describe three EDP controls that are oriented towards protecting an organization's computer system(s).

   1.

   2.

   3.

19. What is the best way to protect your personal privacy?

PROJECTS

1. For each of the controls listed on WORKSHEET 15.1, give a specific example of a procedure that already exists or should be implemented. For the site, use the computer lab or an organization with which you are familiar.

2. Look at the advertisements in several computer or business magazines. Describe two security devices or anti-virus programs that are advertised. Tell where they fit into computer system security.

3. Obtain a blank credit card application, loan application, employment application, or other form requiring personal information. What fields, if any, can be left blank? What fields contain information available through other sources (phone book, employers, etc.)? What fields would you not want available to other family members? potential employers? loan officers? Are there any fields that you don't think are really needed for this application?

4. WHAT DO YOU THINK? Some colleges have open computer labs, where equipment and software are available to anyone capable of using them. In some cases, this includes the community at large and younger school children. Other labs are restricted to students registered for computer-related classes. What are the advantages and disadvantages to both systems? If an open lab is maintained, what additional security measures need to be taken?

5. **WHAT DO YOU THINK?** After reading the signals for computer crime, you probably realize that many of them apply to the place you work or attend school. Should you warn someone if you see one or more of these signals? Who? What could be the positive and negative repercussions of your actions?

WORKSHEETS

15.1 Examples of controls

REFERENCES

Bequai, August. *Technocrime*. Lexington, MS: Lexington Books, 1987.

Compilation of State and Federal Privacy Laws. 6th ed. Providence, RI: Privacy Journal, 1975- (reporting service).

Computer Law Newsletter. Boston, MA: Warner and Stackpole, 1985- (newsletter).

Dreier, Thomas K. "Creation and investment: Artistic and legal implications of computer generated works", *International Computer Law Advisor*, December 90/January 91, pp. 11-23.

Highland, Harold Joseph. "How to prevent the use of weak passwords", *EDP Audit Control and Security Newsletter*, March, 1991, pp. 7-12.

Hruska, Jan. *Computer Viruses and Anti-virus Warfare.* Englewood Cliffs, NJ: 1990.

Johnson, Deborah G. and John W. Snapper. *Ethical Issues in the Use of Computers*. Belmont, CA: Wadsworth, 1985.

Leonard, Peter G. and Waters, Peter. "Copyright or copywrong?", *International Computer Law Advisor*, March, 1991, pp. 4-16.

Stockwell, Thomas M. "Disaster recovery: Starting from scratch", *Information Management*, June, 1991, pp. 91+.

Thimbleby, Harold. "Can viruses ever be useful?", *Computers and Security*, April, 1991, pp. 111-114.

Van Duyn, J. A. *The Human Factor in Computer Crimes*. Princeton, NJ: Petrocelli Books, 1985.

Privacy, Ethics, Crime, and Security

MIX AND MATCH

Match the following terms with the definitions below.
Each question has only one answer.

a. activity log
b. antivirus software
c. control totals
d. copy protection
e. data encryption
f. EDP controls
g. ethical standard
h. password
i. virus
j. write protect
k. write protect notch
l. write protect window

_____ 1. protecting data from overwriting on disk

_____ 2. scrambling data so it cannot be read

_____ 3. procedures for the security of computer systems

_____ 4. record of online transactions

_____ 5. ability to secure data and programs against illegal copying

_____ 6. cutout part of 5.25 inch diskette is covered to prevent overwriting

_____ 7. software used to detect a virus, worm, or other infection on a diskette

_____ 8. code of behavior when dealing with people or situations

_____ 9. sums kept of processed data to compare with hand calculated sums

_____ 10. software that hides inside other software and self-replicates, erasing files as it does.

_____ 11. sliding tab on 3.5 inch diskette that is opened to protect against accidental erasure

_____ 12. code known only to certain users of a system, necessary for access to secured data and programs

Chapter 15

by A. Walters

ACROSS

3. (2nd word with 4 down)

7. Computer program that invades a computer system to erase programs and data files, and can not self-replicate. (pl.)

9. A summary of online activities kept for security purposes.

10. ____ Topology. (1st word). A network with one central computer which has all modes attached only to it. (chpt. 11)

11. Makes interception of electronic mail and other data communications a federal crime. (4 words, 1st word, with 14 down and 16 across)

15. Computer program that invades a computer system from an outside source, is self-contained, and self-replicates until it fills every available memory address.

16. (last 2 words with 11 across and 14 down)

21. Computer program that invades a computer and data files. This type of trouble making program is usually introduced from inside source.

22. Security procedure where errors are detected by comparing independently computed totals with the computer generated equivalent.

24. Scrambling the characters on a disk or transmissions across communication lines to prevent illegal copying of data and programs. (1st word with 26 across)

25. ____ ____ Reporting Act. Citizens can examine information held in their credit files and challenge the data if necessary. (1st word with 1 down)

26. (2nd word with 24 across)

DOWN

1. (2nd word with 25 across)

2. ____ Privacy Protection Act. Prohibits retailers from releasing video-rental data without customer's permission or a court order.

4. A way of storing software on disk which prevents illegal copying by system utilities. (1st word with 3 across)

5. Computer program that invades a computer system by attaching itself to other commonly used programs.

6. Special combination of letters or numbers only known by user that allows access to protected computer systems and files.

8. (chpt. 5) Short line segment added to type style which helps eye flow across line of printed text.

9. Computer program that identifies disk files that have been infected with a virus, worm, or other destructive program. (2 words)

11. ____ Privacy Act. Students can examine and correct errors to their academic records.

12. (chpt. 1) Another word for textual data.

13. Write protect ____. Section cut out of the side of a 5.25-inch floppy disk.

14. (2nd word with 11 across and 16 across)

15. Sliding tab on a 3.5-inch diskette, that can read data from the disk, but it cannot write data on the disk. (1st and 2nd word with 17 down, 3 words)

17. (with 15 down, 3rd word) (pl.)

18. ____ standard. Set of rules a person or organization uses when considering the rights, privileges, and anticipated responses of all persons and groups likely to be affected by a particular action.

19. (chpt. 1) Picture of items on a keyboard.

20. ____ amendment to U.S. Constitution. General rights to privacy, including freedom from unreasonable searches of person, house, papers, and effects.

23. (chpt. 14) High level programming language used in education.

Privacy, Ethics, Crime, and Security

WORKSHEET: 15.1
PROJECT: 1

Name:_____

CONTROL	EXAMPLE
ACCESS TO FACILITIES LIMITED TO AUTHORIZED PEOPLE	
PEOPLE ARE SUPERVISED	
MANUALS ARE SECURE AND AVAILABLE TO USERS	
SCHEDULE OF ACTIVITIES EXIST AND ARE MAINTAINED	
IMPORTANT DATA AND SOFTWARE PROTECTED	
EQUIPMENT PHYSICALLY SECURED	
FACILITIES DESIGNED TO WITHSTAND NATURAL DISASTERS	
SECURE TAPE/DISK LIBRARY	
PROCEDURES EXIST FOR MONITORING EQUIPMENT	
PROCEDURES EXIST FOR KEEPING TRACK OF SOFTWARE	

CLASS NOTES

CHAPTER 16: KEEPING UP WITH CHANGE

PURPOSE

The current technological trends in several areas of society are reviewed in this chapter. They include applications of technology in the global economy, CIM, and consumer electronics. This chapter also surveys the careers paths open to computer professionals as well as opportunities for additional education, professional certification, and a discussion of some of the largest organizations for computer professionals.

TERMS TO REMEMBER

CAD/CAM (computer-aided design/computer-aided manufacturing)
career path
cashless society
computer-aided manufacturing (CAM)
computer architect
computer engineering
computer information systems (CIS)
computer integrated manufacturing (CIM)
computer scientist
conference
continuing education
groupware
human factors engineering
information society
interactive television
just-in-time inventory
materials requirements planning (MRP)
nanomachine
neural network
open systems interconnection (OSI) model
seminar
virtual reality
workshop

ANSWERS TO REVIEW QUESTIONS

1. Define each "term to remember".

   CAD/CAM (computer-aided design/computer-aided manufacturing) -

career path -

cashless society -

computer-aided manufacturing (CAM) -

computer architect -

computer engineering -

computer information systems (CIS) -

computer integrated manufacturing (CIM) -

computer scientist -

conference -

continuing education -

groupware -

human factors engineering -

information society -

interactive television -

just-in-time inventory -

materials requirements planning (MRP) -

nanomachine -

neural network -

open systems interconnection (OSI) model -

seminar -

virtual reality -

workshop -

2. What implications does an information society have on good paying manual labor jobs?

3. How have EFTs helped businesspeople compete in a global economy?

4. What are two shopping services information utilities provide to customers?

   1.

   2.

5. In what ways are robotic applications more advanced than CAM?

6. What is the advantage of creating a computer integrated manufacturing system that follows the OSI model?

7. How do smart homes increase a homeowner's safety and home's energy efficiency?

8. How could information utilities compete with cable television and video tape rental stores?

9. How will optical disk systems make computer games more sophisticated?

10. Describe how a filmless camera works and identify an advantage to creating photographs this way.

11. Describe three applications for interactive television.

    1.

    2.

    3.

12. What are five applications for expert systems at home?

    1.

    2.

    3.

    4.

    5.

13. What are ten applications for embedded computers in cars?

1.	6.
2.	7.
3.	8.
4.	9.
5.	10.

14. Identify two trends for cars of the future.

    1.

    2.

15. What is a good and bad effect of obsolescence for computer professionals and users?

16. Describe the focus of on-the-job training, workshops, and conferences.

17. What is a good way to review professional publications?

18. How has college instruction about computer applications changed over the years?

19. Describe the skills associated with people graduating from college programs in computer information systems, computer science, and computer engineering. Identify classes associated with each area of study.

    computer information systems:

    computer science:

computer engineering:

20. How can a computer professional earn a CDP or CCP?

21. How do professional organizations support personal development?

22. Relate the orientation of the Data Processing Management Association (DPMA), Association for System Managers (ASM), Association for Computing Machinery (ACM), and Institute of Electrical and Electronic Engineers (IEEE) with college programs discussed earlier.

    DPMA -

    ASM -

    ACM -

    IEEE -

23. What are four applications for image processing?

    1.

    2.

    3.

    4.

24. How could you use groupware at part of a project development team?

PROJECTS

1. Use WORKSHEET 16.1 to help you discover your likes and dislikes in a job. Then describe the type of job you would prefer. Find a job advertisement that interests you and list the qualifications needed, experience required, and salary (if known). What experience/education do you still need to acquire to qualify for this job?

2. Many careers involve computers. Investigate your area of interest and discover how computers are used. Organize the information by using the five computer system components (people, procedures, data, software, and hardware).

3. Go to the library and find an article on an emerging technology. Write a short paper explaining the new technology and its potential impact on society.

4. WHAT DO YOU THINK? Interactive television could put you in direct contact with representatives and senators in Congress. Would you take advantage of this opportunity? What effect would it have on government? What would be the advantages and disadvantages of such a system?

WORKSHEETS

16.1 Job preferences

REFERENCES

Bylinsky, Gene. "The marvels of 'virtual reality'", *Fortune*, June 3, 1991, pp. 138-139+.

Carroll, Nick. "Professional freelancing and professional development." *Computer News*, March 1986, p. 7.

CDP Examination Guide. New York: John Wiley and Sons, 1986.

Corcoran, Elizabeth. "Calculating reality", *Scientific American*, January, 1991, pp. 100-109.

Cross, Thomas B. and Marjorie Raizman. *Telecommuting: The Future Technology of Work*. Homewood, IL: Dow Jones-Irwin, 1986.

Dutton, Gail. "Back to school: Trends in training", *computer Operations Manager*, March/April, 1991, pp. 59-60+.

Greenwood, Frank. *Introduction to Computer-Integrated Manufacturing*. San Diego, CA: Harcourt Brace Jovanovich, 1989.

Hall, Alan. "Neural networks: A component of information technology', *Software World*, vol. 22, no. 2, pp. 11-13.

Kochan, D. (Ed.). *CAM: Developments in Computer Integrated Manufacturing*. New York: Springer-Verlag, 1986.

Kuzela, Lad. "A videoconference at your desk?" *Industry Week*, November 24, 1986, p. 72.

McRobbie, Michael A. and Siekmann, Jorg H. "Artificial intelligence: Perspectives and predictions", *Applied AI*, vol. 5, no. 2, pp. 187-207.

Roe, Bill. "Certification: Issues and answers." *Journal of System Management*, July 1984, pp. 3640.

Rudman, Jack. *Computer Specialist: Applications Programming* (Career Examination Series). Syssoset, NY: National Learning Corp.

Rudman, Jack. *Computer Specialist: Database Administrator* (Career Examination Series). Syssoset, NY: National Learning Corp.

Rudman, Jack. *Computer Specialist: Systems Programmer* (Career Examination Series). Syssoset, NY: National Learning Corp.

Toffler, Alvin. *The Third Wave*. New York: Bantam Books, 1980.

Unger, J. Marshal. *The Fifth Generation Fallacy: Why Japan Is Betting the Future on Artificial Intelligence*. New York: Oxford University Press, 1987.

MIX AND MATCH

Match the following terms with the definitions below. Each question has only one answer.

a. CAD/CAM
b. career path
c. cashless society
d. CAM
e. computer architect
f. computer engineering
g. computer information systems
h. CIM
i. computer scientist
j. conference
k. continuing education
l. groupware
m. human factors engineering
n. information society
o. interactive television
p. just-in-time inventory
q. materials requirements planning
r. nanomachine
s. neural network
t. open systems interconnection
u. seminar
v. virtual reality
w. workshop

_____ 1. society where no actual money is exchanged, but all transactions are done electronically

_____ 2. television viewers can communicate with station

_____ 3. computerized inventory to coordinate delivery of raw materials with production schedule

_____ 4. planning the ordering of raw materials and parts to optimize use of production machines

_____ 5. communication between design and manufacturing machines

_____ 6. combination of computerized inventory, MRP, and robotics in a production facility

_____ 7. college major in creating information systems for a variety of applications

_____ 8. college major specializing in development and manufacture of computer hardware

_____ 9. professional educational meeting concentrating on a single topic

_____ 10. designs based on the physical comfort and safety of people

_____ 11. very small machines

241

_____ 12. person designing processing hardware and related systems software

_____ 13. array of processors mimicing neurological conditions

_____ 14. professional education meeting covering a broad subject area

_____ 15. use of programmable machines to control manufacturing

_____ 16. seven tier model for communications standards

_____ 17. person who specializes in systems software design for data and program management

_____ 18. series of jobs followed to reach a career goal

_____ 19. participation in on-the-job-training, workshops, etc.

_____ 20. computer-generated images displaying three dimensional output in goggles and controlled by user's movements

_____ 21. area where people work who depend on information

_____ 22. user interface working in a LAN to support common access to software and data

_____ 23. another name for workshop

Chapter 16

by A. Walters

ACROSS

2. A professional educational meeting concentrating on a single topic that lasts several hours to a few days.

7. A society where all financial transactions are done electronically, based upon an individual's universal account numbers. (2 words)

10. Awarded by the Institute for Certification of Computer Professionals to people who pass a specialized test covering data processing hardware. (abbr.)

12. Computer ____ ____. An area of specialization concerning the creation of systems in business, science, education, and manufacturing. (2 words)

14. Computer ____. Person who specializes in developing techniques for designing system software.

17. Series of related jobs. (1st word with 3 down, 2 words)

22. Participation in on-the-job training, workshops, conferences, or other activities associated with the improvement of job skills.

23. (chpt. 14) High level programming language used in scientific application especially by the Department of Defense.

24. User interface designed to work within a local area network to support common access to application software, office communications, and project data.

25. Use of programmable machines to control manufacturing of products. (abbr.)

26. Seven tier communication standard which promotes connectivity between dissimilar hardware. (abbr.)

28. Extremely small machine.

29. Computer ____. Computer field specializing in the manufacturing, and assembly of hardware.

DOWN

1. (chpt. 6) Intersection of a worksheet row and column containing numbers, formulas, or text.

3. (2nd word with 17 across)

4. (with 12 down, 2nd word)

5. (with 20 down, 2nd word)

6. Awarded by the Institute for Certification of Computer Professionals to people who pass a specialized test covering business, scientific, and systems programming. (abbr.)

8. Computer information ____. Area of specialization concerning the creation of systems in business, science, education, and manufacturing.

9. Parts for assembly or raw materials arrive at a factory before they are needed to minimize storage needed and reduce spoilage of time-dependant products. (4 words, 1st 3 words with 21 down)

11. Existing inventory and production schedules become data for software that schedules ordering and shipment of raw materials. (abbr.)

12. Computer ____ ____. Utilizes the features of CAD/CAM MRP, robotics, and a communications system. (with 4 down, 1st word)

13. Association for ____ ____. Professional organization whose numbers consists of systems personnel. (2 words)

15. Professional organization whose members consists of computer scientists and those involved in computer architecture. (abbr.)

16. Computer ____. Person who specializes in developing processing equipment and associated systems software.

18. (chpt. 14) High level programming language used in education.

19. Professional educational meeting covering a broad subject area.

20. ____ ____ engineering. Designs based on information related to physical comfort and safety. (with 5 down, 1st word)

21. (with 9 down, 4th word)

27. Professional organization whose members consists of computer engineers and architects who design and build computer equipment. (abbr.)

CHAPTER 16

WORKSHEET: 16.1
PROJECT: 1
                                          Name:_____

CAREER IDEAS

AREAS OF INTEREST

LIKES	DISLIKES
INTERESTING JOB TITLES, DUTIES, AND SALARY RANGE	**REQUIRED EXPERIENCE**

244

CLASS NOTES

CLASS NOTES

APPENDIX A: MS AND PC-DOS

PURPOSE

This appendix introduces the microcomputer user to one of the most commonly found disk operating systems, DOS. The booting and formatting operations, as well as the COPY, DIR, DEL, RENAME, MD, CD, and RD commands are discussed.

TERMS TO REMEMBER

active directory
command
data drive
DOS (disk operating system)
DOS prompt
form feed
line feed
MS-DOS
PC-DOS

root disk directory
search path
source drive
subdirectory
switch
system drive
target drive
utility program
volume label

ANSWERS TO REVIEW QUESTIONS

1. Define each "term to remember."

   active directory -

   command -

   data drive -

   disk operating system (DOS) -

   DOS prompt -

   form feed -

APPENDIX A

line feed -

MS-DOS -

PC-DOS -

root disk directory -

search path -

source drive -

subdirectory -

switch -

system drive -

target drive -

utility program -

volume label -

MS and PC-DOS

2. How do you boot an IBM or compatible personal computer?

3. How is the top of page set on a dot matrix printer?

4. What keys are used to output a screen display to the printer?

5. Identify the rules for acceptable DOS filenames.

6. What situation must exist before a DOS utility program can be used?

7. How do you format a new disk?

APPENDIX A

8. What procedure is used to change the system's default disk drive?

9. Explain how you would display the disk directory of any disk in any disk drive.

10. What is the DOS syntax for copying a file from one disk to another keeping the same name? How do you change the name of the duplicate when copying?

11. Explain how to copy a file from one subdirectory to another keeping the same name. How do you change the name of the duplicate when copying?

12. How do you rename existing disk files?

13. Which DOS instructions delete files from disk?

14. How are new subdirectories created on a disk?

15. Explain how you use DOS to change the active disk directory.

16. What is the DOS syntax for removing an existing subdirectory from a disk?

17. Identify the conditions that must exist before a subdirectory can be removed from a disk?

18. What are the common steps for shutting down a microcomputer system?

PROJECTS

1. Make a list of five DOS commands available other than those mentioned in the text. You may find the user's guide for the software helpful. For each command find:

    - what the command does
    - what optional switches are available
    - what abbreviations can be used for the command

2. As mentioned in Chapter 14, software issued by a company undergoes updating. This results in versions of the software. What version of the operating system are you currently using in school? What is the date it was issued? What is the most current version available for that operating system? (Hint: computer magazines will advertise the most current version.)

3. Make up a one-page instruction sheet or poster explaining to a new user how to boot up your machine. Include any diagrams or warnings you think are necessary.

REFERENCES

Busch, David D. *Shareware Plus Featuring 4DOS*. New York: Irwin, 1990.

Dickenson, J. "Forcast for the 90's: the DOS way may still be the best way", *PC Computing*, January, 1991, p. 48.

DOS Workbook and Disks. Carmel, IN: Que Corporation, 1988.

Keough, Lee. "New ways to extend DOS." *Computer Decisions*, March 1988, pp. 28-29.

McMullen, J. "How to get the most out of DOS", *Datamation*, October 1, 1990, pp. 51-52.

Roberts, T. "Introduction to DOS", a series in *Compute!*, starting October, 1990.

Schulman, A. "DOS unbound: Use of protected mode", *Byte Fall 1990 IBM Special Edition*, pp. 250-256.

Schulman, A. "Undocumented DOS", *Byte*, March, 1991, pp. 287-288+.

Trainor, Timothy N. and Jeffrey Stipes. *A Guide To MS/PC DOS*. Santa Cruz, CA: Mitchell Publishing, 1989.

Voneig, D. C. *DOS Tips, Tricks, and Traps*. Carmel, IN: Que Corporation, 1989.

Wrona, Thomas. *How to Run a Hard Disk PC*. Glenview, IL: Scott, Foresman, 1988.

MIX AND MATCH

Match the following terms with the definitions below.
Each question has only one answer.

a. active directory
b. command
c. data drive
d. DOS
e. DOS prompt
f. form feed
g. line feed
h. MS-DOS
i. PC-DOS
j. root disk directory
k. search path
l. source drive
m. subdirectory
n. switch
o. system drive
p. target drive
q. volume label

_____ 1. disk operating system developed by Microsoft, Inc.

_____ 2. directory DOS uses as a default

_____ 3. DOS instruction that can be executed at any time

_____ 4. the destination drive in a copy command

_____ 5. button on printer moving paper one line at a time

_____ 6. directory added to disk after root directory is created

_____ 7. primary disk directory created when disk is formatted

_____ 8. symbols like A> showing the computer is ready for user instructions

_____ 9. button on printer moving paper one page at a time

_____ 10. drive DOS uses to read programs or data

_____ 11. disk operating system

_____ 12. description of how to find a subdirectory or file by identifying disk drive and file location

_____ 13. drive that reads the DOS disk

_____ 14. option available with a DOS instruction

APPENDIX A

_____ 15. user defined name given to a diskette when it is formatted

_____ 16. drive used to store application programs and data files

_____ 17. DOS version distributed by IBM

APPENDIX B: MICROSOFT WINDOWS

PURPOSE

This appendix is a hands-on tutorial covering the basic operations of Microsoft Windows including formatting a disk, manipulating windows, and copying files.

TERMS TO REMEMBER

boot disk
clicking
control box
context sensitive
data drive
desktop
DOS prompt
dragging
folder
menu bar
MS-DOS

PC-DOS
pointer
root disk directory
scroll arrow
scroll bar
scroll box
search path
system drive
title bar
volume label
Windows

ANSWERS TO REVIEW QUESTIONS

1. Define each "term to remember".

    boot disk -

    clicking -

    control box -

    context sensitive -

    data drive -

    desktop -

APPENDIX B

DOS prompt -

dragging -

folder -

menu bar -

MS-DOS -

PC-DOS -

pointer -

root disk directory -

scroll arrow -

scroll bar -

scroll box -

search path -

system drive -

title bar -

volume label -

Windows -

2. How do you boot an IBM or compatible personal computer?

3. How do you load and run Windows?

4. Explain what is meant by the desktop metaphor.

5. Explain how an icon can be moved around the desktop.

6. Describe how an option is selected from a pull-down menu.

7. Why are some menu option dimmer than others?

8. What are three ways to open a window?

   1.

   2.

   3.

9. Describe four ways to alter the size of a window.

   1.

   2.

   3.

   4.

10. How do you deactivate a window?

11. How do you format a new disk using Windows?

12. How are folders used in the desktop?

13. Explain how you would use Windows to display the disk directory of any disk in any disk drive.

14. What windows, menus, and icons are used to copy a file from one disk to another keeping the same name? How do you change the name of the duplicate when copying?

15. Identify the rules for acceptable DOS/Windows filenames.

16. How do you rename an existing disk file using Windows?

17. Explain how you would use Windows to delete files from disk?

18. How are new subdirectories created on a disk using Windows?

19. Explain how to copy a file from one file folder to another keeping the same name. How do you change the name of the duplicate when copying?

20. Identify the conditions that must exist before a subdirectory can be removed from a disk?

21. How do you use Windows to remove an existing subdirectory folder from a disk?

22. What are the common steps for shutting down a microcomputer system?

PROJECTS

1. Make a list of five Windows operations available other than those mentioned in the text. You may find the user's guide for the software helpful. For each command find:

   - what the operation does
   - what menu options are used to initiate this action
   - what alternative keystrokes can initiate this action

2. As mentioned in Chapter 14, software issued by a company undergoes updating. This results in versions of the software. What version of Windows are you currently using in school? What is the date it was issued? What is the most current version available for that operating system? (Hint: computer magazines will advertise the most current version.)

3. Make up a one-page instruction sheet or poster explaining to a new user a specific Windows operation. Include any diagrams or warnings you think are necessary.

REFERENCES

English, A. V. "Legacy for Windows", *Home Office Computing*, August 1991, p. 53.

Kolowich, M. E. "Where are the business benefits of Windows?", *PC Computing*, February, 1991, p. 13.

Lubeck, J. H. and Schatzman, D. "Making Windows work", *Byte*, January, 1991, pp. 293-296+.

Minase, M. "Windows tips and tricks", *Byte*, May, 1991, pp. 328+.

Moad, Jeff. "What's wrong with Windows?", *Datamation*, April 1, 1991, pp. 43-44.

Morganstern, S. "Windows 3.0: What's in it for you?", *Home Office Computing*, January, 1991, pp. 47-51.

Smith, G. "Windows 3.1 is the first step, but what's the future of GUIs?", *PC Computing*, May, 1991, pp. 50-51.

Weiskamp, Keith and Aguiar, Saul. *Windows 3.0: A Self-Teaching Guide*. New York: John Wiley & Sons, 1991.

"Windows", *PC Computing* (cover story and special section), April, 1991, pp. 34-37+.

"Windows 3.0 shortcuts", *PC Computing*, January, 1991, pp. 171-172 and February, 1991, pp. 183-184.

Yip, Stephen W. L. and Robson, David J. "Window user interfaces and software maintenance", *Journal of Software Maintenance*, June, 1991, pp. 107-123.

Microsoft Windows

MIX AND MATCH

Match the following terms with the definitions below.
Each question has only one answer.

a. boot disk
b. clicking
c. control box
d. context sensitive
e. data drive
f. desktop
g. DOS prompt
h. dragging
i. folder
j. menu bar
k. MS-DOS

l. PC-DOS
m. pointer
n. root disk directory
o. scroll arrow
p. scroll bar
q. scroll box
r. search path
s. system drive
t. title bar
u. volume label
v. Windows

_____ 1. horizontal area running across top of window displaying titles of menus

_____ 2. horizontal area across top of window displaying window's title

_____ 3. box used to deactivate a window

_____ 4. screen display with letter and greater than sign indicating default drive

_____ 5. directions on how to find a file by giving drive name and directory location

_____ 6. cursor controlled by a mouse

_____ 7. disk with DOS that must be in a drive to start system

_____ 8. user assigned name given to a diskette when it is formatted

_____ 9. using pointer to move an icon to another area of the screen

_____ 10. area of window containing scroll box and scroll arrows

_____ 11. disk operating system distributed by IBM

_____ 12. help screen pertains directly to area of window that was designated

APPENDIX B

_____ 13. screen setup associated with a GUI showing tools and options similar to those found on a desk

_____ 14. directory created when a diskette is formatted

_____ 15. disk drive containing DOS

_____ 16. icon used by a GUI that represents a subdirectory

_____ 17. pressing button on a mouse to initiate an action

_____ 18. GUI software available from Microsoft Corp.

_____ 19. DOS available from Microsoft Corp.

_____ 20. area in scroll bar showing which portion of the window is presently being viewed

_____ 21. drive containing disk with applications and data files

_____ 22. area of scroll bar clicked on to change the view of a window

APPENDIX C: APPLE MACINTOSH

PURPOSE

This appendix introduces the basic commands and techniques used to operate an Apple Macintosh microcomputer. Included in this hands-on tutorial are formatting a disk, copying files, and manipulating windows and icons.

TERMS TO REMEMBER

clicking
close box
desktop
dragging
external diskette drive
folder
internal diskette drive

menu bar
pointer
scroll arrow
scroll bar
scroll box
title bar

ANSWERS TO REVIEW QUESTIONS

1. Define each "term to remember."

    clicking -

    close box -

    desktop -

    dragging -

    external diskette drive -

    folder -

APPENDIX C

internal diskette drive -

menu bar -

pointer -

scroll arrow -

scroll bar -

scroll box -

title bar -

2. What are the hardware components for a Macintosh system?

3. Describe the start-up procedure for a Macintosh system.

4. Explain what is meant by the desktop metaphor.

5. What is the purpose of the trashcan icon?

6. Explain how an icon can be moved around the desktop.

7. How is a new diskette initialized?

8. What are the rules for naming an item on the Macintosh system?

9. Describe how an option is selected from a pull-down menu.

10. What are three ways to open a window?

    1.

    2.

    3.

11. What information is contained in a window's title bar?

12. Describe two ways to alter the size of a window.

    1.

    2.

13. How are folders used in the desktop?

14. Which menu option allows the user to create folders?

15. Explain how a folder or icon can be renamed.

16. Which menu option is used to make a copy of an object within a window?

17. How is an object moved from one window to another?

18. What is the procedure for shutting down the system?

PROJECTS

1. Make a list of five Macintosh desktop operations available other than those mentioned in the text. You may find the user's guide for the software helpful. For each command find:

   - what the operation does
   - what menu options are used to initiate this action
   - what alternative keystrokes can initiate this action

2. As mentioned in Chapter 14, software issued by a company undergoes updating. This results in versions of the software. What version of the Macintosh desktop are you currently using in school? What is the date it was issued? What is the most current version available for that operating system? (Hint: computer magazines will advertise the most current version.)

3. Make up a one-page instruction sheet or poster explaining to a new user a specific Macintosh operation. Include any diagrams or warnings you think are necessary.

REFERENCES

"A wallet-friendly Macintosh that delivers performance", *Byte*, March, 1991, pp. 257-258+.

Cisler, S. "The new Macintosh: priced for library budgets", *Online*, January, 1991, pp. 75-77.

Crabb, D. E. "Working with Windows 3.0 and a Macintosh", *Byte*, November, 1990, pp. 107-108+.

Kawasaki, Guy. *The Macintosh Way.* Glenview, IL: Scott Foresman, 1989.

Lu, C. "Macs or IBMs: How to weigh the choice between buying a PC or a Macintosh", *Inc.*, January, 1991, pp. 116+.

MacMenu: A Menu Information Directory for Macintosh Computers. New York: Menu Publishers, 1990.

Pepper, J. "A bushel of new apples [Macintosh computers, printers and hardware]", *Nation's Business*, March 1991, pp. 38-40.

MIX AND MATCH

Match the following terms with the definitions below.
Each question has only one answer.

a. clicking
b. close box
c. desktop
d. dragging
e. external diskette drive
f. folder
g. internal diskette drive

h. menu bar
i. pointer
j. scroll arrow
k. scroll bar
l. scroll box
m. title bar

_____ 1. horizontal area running across top of window displaying titles of menus

_____ 2. horizontal area across top of window displaying window's title

_____ 3. box used to deactivate a window

_____ 4. drive built into the main computer unit

_____ 5. cursor controlled by a mouse

_____ 6. using pointer to move an icon to another area of the screen

_____ 7. area of window containing scroll box and scroll arrows

_____ 8. screen setup associated with a GUI showing tools and options similar to those found on a desk

_____ 9. icon used by a GUI that represents a subdirectory

_____ 10. pressing button on a mouse to initiate an action

_____ 11. drive connected by cable outside of the main computer unit

_____ 12. area in scroll bar showing which portion of the window is presently being viewed

_____ 13. area of scroll bar clicked on to change the view of a window

APPENDIX D: BASIC

PURPOSE

This appendix serves as a hands-on tutorial for learning many of the statements and commands in the BASIC programming language. Structured programming techniques are examined. Also, a comparison is made between batch programs and interactive programs.

TERMS TO REMEMBER

command	nonexecutable statement
echo-printing	print zone
error messages	sentinel value
expression	statement
fixed point constant	string variable
infinite loop	syntax
integer constant	TAB
key word	trailer value
logical operator	variable

BASIC COMMANDS

CLS	LOAD
KEY OFF	NEW
KEY ON	RUN
LIST	SAVE
LLIST	

BASIC STATEMENTS

DATA	LET
END	LPRINT
FOR...NEXT	PRINT
GOTO	READ
IF-THEN	REM
INPUT	

APPENDIX D

ANSWERS TO REVIEW QUESTIONS

1. Define each "term to remember".

   command -

   echo-printing -

   expression -

   fixed point constant -

   infinite loop -

   integer constant -

   keyword -

   logical operator -

   nonexecutable statement -

   print zone -

   sentinel value -

statement -

string variable -

syntax -

TAB -

trailer value -

variable -

2. For which type of users was BASIC designed?

3. How is the BASIC translator loaded from disk different from the translator loaded from ROM?

4. What procedure do you use to load the BASIC translator into the computer's memory?

5. Describe the function of each "BASIC command" listed below.

   CLS -

   KEY OFF -

   KEY ON -

   LIST -

   LLIST -

   LOAD -

   NEW -

   RUN -

   SAVE -

6. How are BASIC statements different from BASIC commands?

7. Describe the function of each "BASIC statement" listed below.

DATA -

END -

FOR...NEXT -

GOTO -

IF-THEN -

INPUT -

LET -

LPRINT -

PRINT -

READ -

REM -

APPENDIX D

8. What are the flowcharting symbols for start, input, processing, decision, output, and end?

   start -

   input -

   processing -

   decision -

   output -

   end -

9. How do you correct an error before and after a program instruction is entered into memory?

10. Why are the line numbers in a BASIC program usually incremented by 10?

11. Where must a space be inserted in a BASIC statement?

12. What does the computer display on the screen when it is waiting for the user to input data?

13. What are the rules for naming a BASIC program?

14. Identify which characters are acceptable for numeric constants and which characters are not acceptable?

15. How long can a variable name be?

16. How are parentheses used in a BASIC expression?

17. What is the hierarchy of arithmetic operations in BASIC?

   1.

   2.

   3.

   4.

18. How can a user get out of an infinite loop?

19. What are the default print zones in BASIC?

20. How is the output different when semicolons are used instead of colons to separate items in a BASIC PRINT statement?

21. How are headings created as output from a BASIC program?

22. What criterion is used to select a trailer (sentinel) value?

23. What are the six logical operators used in BASIC IF...THEN statements?

   1.

   2.

   3.

   4.

   5.

   6.

24. Explain how totals are accumulated and at what point in the program execution they are usually printed.

25. What distinguishes a string variable name from a numeric variable name?

26. Why do programmers use graph paper or a print chart to design a report before writing the program?

27. How long (number of characters) can a BASIC statement be?

28. What happens when a semicolon is placed at the end of a PRINT statement?

29. What distinguishes a string value from a numeric value?

30. How do you separate multiple INPUT values entered on the same line?

31. What are nested FOR...NEXT loops?

32. How can a programmer place more than one BASIC statement on the same line?

33. Why would a programmer want to place each statement on its own line and include REM statements?

PROJECTS

1. Code a BASIC program to produce a listing of the birthdays and anniversaries of your friends and relatives. Input should consist of the name, date, and whether it is an anniversary or birthday.

2. Code a BASIC program to construct a table listing textbook information for any student at your school. Input might consist of anything from one to 20 or more books. Each input item should consist of the book title, author, course it is used for, and the cost of the book. Assume you can sell used books for 3/4 of what you paid for them. Your output should consist of all of the inputs, plus the price you can sell the books for. Output also should include the totals of both the prices you paid, and the selling prices when you resell them.

3. You have been needing a new car and you have collected information on a number of possibilities. You have listed the make, model, year and price for each car. You also have collected data on the down payment necessary to purchase each car, and the number and amount of the monthly payments. Code a BASIC program to display all of this information, as well as the difference between the price of the car and the sum of the monthly payments plus the down payment.

4. Code a BASIC program that will input information about the courses a student takes. This would vary between one and perhaps seven or eight for the real Einsteins at your school. Input data would include the course title, the number of credit hours, the day(s) it meets, the time of the class meeting, the building designation, and the room number. Your output report should include the student name and Social Security number, all of the other input listed above, and the total number of course hours taken.

The emphasis behind the next set of exercises is the use of the FOR...NEXT statements.

5. You have a part-time job with hours varying from a low of ten hours per week, to a high of 25 hours per week. Code a BASIC program that will INPUT your rate of pay per hour, and produce a table showing your gross income for the number of hours worked, from 10 to 25 in quarter-hour intervals.

6. Code a BASIC program, using nested FOR...NEXT loops that will produce a calendar for the current month. Then, modify your program so that it can handle ANY month, for which the number of days in the month and the day on which the first of the month falls, are INPUT.

7. Code a BASIC program that will produce a temperature conversion table, for all temperatures between freezing and boiling. Your program should ask the user if an F- to -C conversion table, or a C- to -F conversion table is desired. Your table should be printed with PRINT USING statements, rounding to a tenth of a degree.

8. Code a BASIC program that will produce a kilometer-to-miles or a miles-to-kilometers table, depending upon the wishes of the user. Your table should run from 1 to 100 kilometers or miles and include appropriate headings. Output should be printed with the PRINT USING statement, rounded to tenths.

REFERENCES

Boggs, Roy A. *Advanced BASIC for the IBM PC*. Englewood Cliffs, NJ: Prentice-Hall, 1986.

Campbell, T. "BASIC is back", *Compute!*, February, 1991, pp. 64-66+.

Campbell, T. "Mover over Microsoft, here's PowerBASIC", *Compute!*, June, 1991, pp. 73-74.

Davis, William S. *PC BASIC: Getting Started*. Rading, MA: Addison-Wesley, 1987.

Downing. *Computer BASIC the Easy Way (2nd ed.)*. New York: Maron, 1989.

Fox, Anne. *Armchair BASIC: An Absolute Beginner's Guide to Programming in BASIC.*, New York: Osborne McGraw, 1988.

Kemeny, J. G. and Kurtz, T. E. "On BASIC", *Byte*, September, 1990, p. 276.

Lien, David A. *The BASIC Handbook: Encyclopedia of the BASIC Programming Language*. San Diego, CA: CompuSoft Publishing, 1986.

Norton, Peter. *Peter Norton's Advanced BASIC.* Englewood Cliffs, NJ: Prentice Hall, 1991.

Norton, Peter. *Peter Norton's BASIC On-Line Guide.* New York: Brady Books, 1990.

Shammas, Namir Clement. *The New BASICS: Programming Techniques and Library Development.* Redwood City, CA: M & T Books, 1987.

Simpson, Henry. *Serious Programming in BASIC.* Blue Ridge Summit, PA: TAB Books, 1986.

BASIC

MIX AND MATCH

Match the following terms with the definitions below.
Each question has only one answer.

I. TERMS TO REMEMBER

a. command
b. echo-printing
c. error message
d. expression
e. fixed point constant
f. infinite loop
g. integer constant
h. key word
i. logical operator
j. nonexecutable statement
k. print zone
l. sentinel value
m. string variable
n. syntax
o. TAB function
p. trailer value
q. variable

_____ 1. screen displays what user has input

_____ 2. variable containing alphanumeric data

_____ 3. symbols to the right of the equal sign in a LET statement

_____ 4. statement that is ignored by the computer

_____ 5. important word that must be included in a command or statement

_____ 6. constant consisting only of numbers and plus/minus signs, no decimal points

_____ 7. BASIC option that controls tabulation on a line

_____ 8. name that can represent a variety of values

_____ 9. area of paper, 14 columns wide, that is the default printing area for BASIC

_____ 10. <, < =, >, > =, =, and < >

_____ 11. constant containing numbers, plus/minus sign, and a decimal point

_____ 12. instruction that is immediately executed by BASIC

_____ 13. another name for trailer value

_____ 14. the grammar of a programming language

_____ 15. last data value triggering the end of a loop

_____ 16. loop that continuously repeats

_____ 17. statement displayed listing a program bug

II. BASIC COMMANDS

a. CLS
b. KEY OFF
c. KEY ON
d. LIST
e. LLIST

f. LOAD
g. NEW
h. RUN
i. SAVE

_____ 1. display program statements on the screen

_____ 2. copy a program from diskette into the computer's memory

_____ 3. copy a program from the computer's memory onto diskette

_____ 4. execute a series of BASIC statements

_____ 5. remove function key line at bottom of screen

_____ 6. restore function key line at bottom of screen

_____ 7. print program statements on paper

_____ 8. clear screen without changing memory

_____ 9. clears the program from the computer's memory

III. BASIC STATEMENTS

a. DATA
b. END
c. FOR...NEXT
d. GOTO
e. IF...THEN
f. INPUT
g. LET
h. LPRINT
i. PRINT
j. READ
k. REM

_____ 1. allows user to enter data in batch mode

_____ 2. decision statement

_____ 3. allows arithmetic computations to be done

_____ 4. counting loop

_____ 5. nonexecutable statement

_____ 6. prints output on paper

_____ 7. assigns data in DATA statements to listed variables

_____ 8. last statement executed in a BASIC program

_____ 9. allows user to enter data interactively

_____ 10. displays output on a screen

_____ 11. transfers control to a given statement number

CLASS NOTES

CLASS NOTES

CLASS NOTES

CLASS NOTES

CLASS NOTES

CLASS NOTES

CLASS NOTES

CLASS NOTES

CLASS NOTES

CLASS NOTES

CLASS NOTES

CLASS NOTES

CLASS NOTES